EXTREME
Muscle Cars
The Factory Lightweight Legacy

Bill Holder & Phil Kunz
Forewords by Dick Brannan, Arnie Beswick & Hayden Proffitt

©2006 Bill Holder & Phil Kunz
Published by

An Imprint of F+W Publications

700 East State Street • Iola, WI 54990-0001
715-445-2214 • 888-457-2873

Our toll-free number to place an order or obtain
a free catalog is (800) 258-0929.

Library of Congress Catalog Number: 2005935071

ISBN 13-digit: 978-0-89689-278-1
ISBN 10-digit: 0-89689-278-6

Designed by Tom Nelsen
Edited by Tom Collins

Printed in United States of America

DEDICATION

To the late "Dyno Don" Nicholson, as well as James "Hammer" Mason

Don Nicholson epitomized the lightweight era as a driver and engine builder. His "Dyno" nickname came from the fact that he was the first to use a chassis dyno for drag racing. Don raced with NHRA but a majority of his drag racing was done in match race competitions where he won 90 percent of the time. He competed in Super Stock, Factory Experimental and in Funny Cars. He drove cars from all of the Big Three manufacturers. He was a true legend of the sport.

ACKNOWLEDGMENTS

Thanks to the following for allowing the photographing of their cars: Wally Abella, Earl Brown, Joe Cochran, Colon Comer, Tony DePillo, Mike Garblic, Mike Guarise, David Greene, Brent Hajek, Rick Johnson Harold Leiter, Michael Moore, Mike Pierce, Dr. I. Russo, Steve Snyder, Jim Wangers, and Jack Werst.

Technical assistance data from Arnie Beswick, Dick Brannan, Brian Coleman, Charles Crites, Greg Donohue, Dan Fuller, Mike Garblik, George Gudat, Bill "Grumpy" Jenkins, Hayden Proffitt, Jeff Skunkart, Doug Thorley, David Tom, and Jim Wangers.

Photo Support: John Beecroft, Arnie Beswick, Jack Biel, Dick Brannan, Brian Colement, John Craft, Charles and France Crites, Scott Dahlberg, John Durand, Ray English/Draglist.com, Bill Erdman, Dan Fuller, Joe Germann, Tom Glatch, George Gudat, the Phil Hall Collection, Craig Handley, P. J. Heck, Johnny Kelly, Mark Long, Greg Mancini, Bob McClurg, Elton McFall, Todd Miller, Tom Molyneaux, Mike Moore, Mike Mueller, Patrick Paternie, Bob Pickel, Bob and Dorothy Plumer of Drag Racing Memories, Bill Pratt, David Tom, Jeanne Weiss, and Jean Williams.

CONTENTS

INTRODUCTION

All other things being equal, the lighter vehicle will win in any type of motor competition. That was really the case in drag racing as the innovation of the lightweight drag car proved during the 1960s.

It was an unbelievable time period when the factories built, or contracted out, full-race lightweight drag cars. They weren't generally street legal and were basically built for the professional drag race teams of the national series.

The lightweight phenomenon certainly came as a result of the build-up in performance in the late 1950s and early 1960s. It came from all the manufacturers with Ford showing several potent versions of its 312 engine, including a 340 horsepower NASCAR version carrying a Paxton supercharger. There would also be a 352-cid engine capable of 300 horsepower with a single four-barrel carburetor.

The Mercury Division also had some big horsepower numbers with a 383 engine capable of 330 horsepower and a monster 430-cid big block with 360 ponies being pumped out.

In 1957, Chevy introduced its vaunted 283-cid fuel-injected engine that was capable of the same number of horses. There was also a 348-cid Tri-Power engine that pounded down 335 horses. Pontiac was certainly not to be left behind with a powerful 370-cid engine with 285 horsepower or 300 horsepower.

MOPAR was also right in the under-the-hood category with powerful engines available to both the Plymouth and Dodge models.

Mike Mueller

For Dodge, the D500 354 engine provided 340 horsepower and was equipped with a pair of Carter four-barrel carburetors. There was also a 361 cubic inch power plant that was rated at 345 horses with fuel injection. For Plymouth, there was the Golden Commando engine that showed a 305-hp value. Even AMC was putting down some very impressive horsepower.

All well and good, and with a skilled engine man, those impressive figures could be boosted to even higher levels. But there was an unavoidable situation that was faced by the drag teams that would limit the performance of the vehicles.

Quite simply, it was the WEIGHT of the period machines that really held things up for better performance. Most of them were in the 3,500-pound or heavier category, and some were pushing the two-ton weight. That's a lot of iron to push down the quarter mile, and the engines were putting out about as much as was feasibly possible.

One logical answer remained. Lighten up the cars and you had to go faster. It was as simple as that! And during the 1960s, an amazing set of circumstances took place, in a decade that most certainly has to rate as the most exciting in American drag racing history.

Some of the prominent models selected for the early 1960s factory lightweight applications were the Chevy Impala and Biscayne, the Pontiac Catalina, the Dodge Coronet and Dart, the Plymouth Belvedere and Savoy models, and the Ford Galaxie and Mustang. Also involved were the

Mike Mueller

Mercury and its Comet and Cyclone, and AMC with its AMX.

The cars ran mostly in two classes, Super Stock and Factory Experimental. The Super Stock Class served as the basis for the popular Pro Stock Class that would follow in the 1970s. Some of the Factory Experimental cars, called Altered Wheelbase cars, actually had the location of the wheels changed for more rear-end weight. They were basically the first Funny Cars. These cars participated in the wildly-popular match races and used nitro fuel and superchargers.

Also recall, for the most part, these lightweight cars started out as real street vehicles, and not the tubular chassis' hand-built machines of today. During the end of the 1960s, though, the beginnings of modern high-tech began.

There were so many different lightening techniques attempted, some that were very successful, and others that just work out. Some were simple, and some were quite complex.

One of the simplest techniques was drilling holes in solid metal pieces that reduced the weight of the object, but certainly had a negative effect on its strength. Also, there were certain lightweights that had their complete frame totally dipped in acid, reducing the thickness of the material. Others just used thinner metal from the beginning.

There was also the considerable substitution of aluminum parts replacing the factory steel pieces. That consisted of such items as bumpers and even sheet metal panels. But aluminum wasn't the only lightening material used, as there was also an early use of fiberglass in body panels, or using the strong, light material for the complete body shell.

Plexiglass was often substituted for window glass, and even heaters, radios, and the window roll-up mechanisms were deleted.

With the aluminum and thinner steel components, one had better not lean on a fender, as it was easily possible to dent the leaned-on area. Finally, there was sometimes the use of aluminum in the engines, both for a lighter power plant and one with possible higher performance.

There was an easier way to loose weight, being the technique of using lighter factory models. That was certainly done by Chrysler with its use of the barebones Savoy and Belvedere models. Using the Chevy II and Ford Falcon allowed the trimming of some 400 pounds without having to cut that first piece of metal.

Now granted, the factory lightweight cars received a majority of the attention, but those were not the only lightweights that roamed the nation's drag strips. A number of the teams built light cars on their own, with excellent results on the track.

Many of these cars copied the factory versions. When the "Factory Lightweight" terminology of these cars is used, there is a fine line on determining where it started and ended. For this book, the definition would be when the factories were involved, either from a fabrication or a money-involvement in the cars.

With that set of rules, the start point for the era took place in the early 1960s time period with the termination occurring during the 1969 time period. There were periods, though, when some companies withdrew from the activity.

There were huge driver names during the lightweight era with the likes of Arnie Beswick, Dick Landy, Jack Chrisman, Phil Bonner, Dick Brannan, Gas Ronda, Hubert Platt, Sox and Martin, and numerous others.

It was a time that the companies realized the value of automotive performance in the marketing and selling of the their particular product. It wasn't uncommon to see the likes of Nicholson, Brannan, and Beswick appearing in national factory advertisements that praised their accomplishments on the drag strip. With the muscle cars of the era, the lightweights served as a perfect fit for advertising them.

Probably more than any other time period, this was really the "Win on Sunday, sell on Monday" phenomenon at its best. Bet there were those that bought the same street version of a lightweight drag car, and then wondered why their machine couldn't come within three or four seconds of the time run by the lights. It should be noted, though, that with certainly lightweight models, some of the cars could be bought off the showroom floor.

Imagine this scenario. The car companies were actually building race-ready drag machines that could be taken directly to the drag strip and put into action. Really, this is actually what happened! It's hard to imagine in today's world, with all its regulations and environmental considerations that

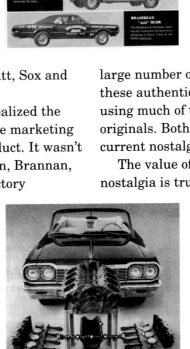

such activity would ever be allowed.

It was much more radical than the NASCR racecar activity that took place in the latter part of the 1960s decade. During that time period, Ford and Chrysler actually built five models that were intended to qualify for NASCAR racing. But the difference with these machines—the Dodge Daytona and Charger 500, the Plymouth Superbird, the Ford Talladega and Mercury Spoiler II— were built for the street, and were modified by the teams for actually raced. They were all quite streetable and were all street legal.

The mystic of that era lives over four decades later as many of these vintage drag cars have been retrieved and brought back to their racing trim. Also, there have been a large number of replicas made of the cars. Many of these authentic-looking machines were constructed using much of the same componentry as the originals. Both are displayed and campaigned in current nostalgic racing events.

The value of the original cars in this area of nostalgia is truly amazing, on occasion reaching and surpassing the six-figure level. Of course, the fact that the numbers of these cars was so minimal also plays heavily to their present value.

For example, in the 2005 Barrett-Jackson Auction, an original '65 Dodge Super Stock Lightweight brought $192,500!! Even the replicas are bringing amazing figures.

Even today, the atmosphere of that fabulous time still lives. You might call in the "Lightweight Look" with small or no wheel covers, Super Stock-style hood scoops, and radio/heater delete. Ultra-powerful engines, super-light bodies, the nation's top drag racing drivers, it was an era that will never be repeated again.

One final note needs to be stated for purposes of production numbers of these various lightweight cars. For some of them, there are discrepancies on the numbers produced. For this book, when possible, the range of numbers in existence, will be quoted. ◆

Chapter 1

AMC
LIGHTWEIGHTS

A late start. A short tenure. That's the way you would have to describe the lightweight drag racing adventure of the American Motors Corporation.

But the company considered that starting late was better than doing nothing. After all, this was the muscle car era and the other companies were turning out performance models that were selling well. With its econobox image, it figured that it just had to join the factory-supported drag race arena, which was enjoying a high visibility during the late-1960s period.

There was some history in putting Ramblers and speed together, despite their reputation as economy cars. Some 1,500 1957 Ramblers got a 255-hp V-8 that turned them into lightweight screamers called Rebels. *Motor Trend* reported a 7.5-second clocking for the Rebel four-door hardtop while *Hot Rod* recorded a 9.4-second time. It was a story that turned heads for those used to stories in the '50s about a Nash or a Rambler excelling in economy, not speed.

A Javelin dragster that was driven by Marvin Eldredge.

In 1963, *Hot Rod* reported on a drag racing Rambler Ambassador 880 two-door sedan sponsored by Dell-Kraft Rambler of Norwalk,

Bob Plumer

This car originally served as the "mule" for the SS/AMX. Currently, it is owned by Garrett Ghezzi and is still campaigned in nostalgia drag racing.

Garrett Ghezzi Collection

California. Service manager Preston Honea was winning trophies in D/ Stock Automatic competitions. While the Ambassador 880 was a beefy Rambler, the car's 3,108-pound weight was lighter than many. It ran with an automatic transmission, slightly modified for the drag strip, plus Twin-Grip differential, and station wagon coil springs.

The block was bored to .30 and heads were milled .018. Add-ons included Monroe Load Leveler shocks, NGK plugs, a modified torque converter, plus Horsepower Engineering headers. This was one car from Kenosha that reached 97 mph in just over 14 seconds and was getting faster all the time! An advantage for the Rambler was its unibody construction, lighter than the body-on-frame cars. And the Dell-Kraft car did get the Rambler name in competition. Apparently the factory noticed.

In just a few short years, there were a certain number of machines that would have served as starting points for a Super Stock drag machine. One

was selected, but it might not have been the one you would have figured.

Through that same period, though, AMC already was involved with several models that could have been considered as candidates for a lightweight factory drag machine. They were the 69-1/2 AMC/Hurst

RON ROOT, Driver

Phil Hall Collection

Ron Root drove the Southern California Javelin.

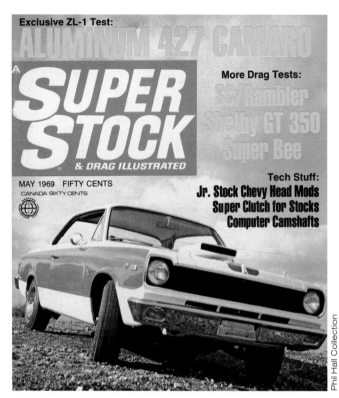

Phil Hall Collection

The AMC SC/Rambler was the Super Stock *cover car in May 1969.*

SC/Rambler, the 1970 Rebel Machine, and finally the winner, the 1969 AMX. That latter model would be the model selected for this interesting experiment.

But those first two models certainly had the potential to have fulfilled the goal, and they certainly deserve a mention.

The SC/Rambler

In stock trim, the SC/Rambler looked like it belonged in competition. It was a machine that was modified extensively by Hurst. First, it was a dazzling red, white, and blue hauler of which only 1,512 were built. The model weighed in at a moderate 3,160 pounds and was powered by a 390-cid/315-horse V-8 that produced 425 lbs.-ft. of torque. It carried a single Carter AFB four-barrel carb. With its raised, macho hood scoop, it had the look of a race car. The SC/Rambler carried its racing look well and also included an 8,000 rpm tachometer, glass pack mufflers, blue Magnum 500 wheels and wore Goodyear Polyglas E70 x 14 redline tires.

The remainder of the power train consisted of the Hurst-shifted four-speed manual transmission, and a 3.54 rear end. In the quarter mile, it did a respectable 14.14 seconds at 100 mph. It has also showed well at the local drag strips, but nothing at the national level.

Automobile Quarterly writer Mike Covello wrote: "[AMC Chairman Roy] Abernethy attempted to make the solid citizen into a swinger suitable for those seeking a sporty compact."

Car buffs quickly combined the letters and simply called the car the "Scrambler" and the name fit with all its Hurst add-ons, the AMC 390-cid V-8 and its affordable $2,998 price.

Additional pieces on the SC/Rambler were a column-mounted Sun 8,000-rpm tach, Thrush glass pack mufflers (that apparently didn't muffle much), and a Borg-Warner T-10 transmission coupled with the famed Hurst floor-mounted four-speed shifter. The package weighed in at just 3,160 lbs.

AMC hit the drag racing audience with ads that screamed "It Only Hurts Them for 14 Seconds." One publication put the SC/Rambler through its paces and found it could travel the quarter mile in just 12.6 seconds.

There were three lots of 500 each of the SC/Rambler. The first 500 had an all white body with red lower sides and a blue stripe down the center of the car. The second 500 carried a blue racing stripe the length of the car and the lower sides were painted blue. The third lot of 512 cars was like the first group. There were 512 SC/Ramblers produced in the final group including 10 that went to the James Garner-backed American International Racing (AIR) team.

An AMC SC/Rambler definitely was AMC fun!

The way it was garnished up with a red, white, and blue race-looking paint design wouldn't have looked out of place on a national drag strip. And it could have been even wilder. There are reports that AMC built at least two four-wheel-drive versions of the SC/Rambler in its final lot of 512 cars!

The Rebel Machine

In a 1968 ad, American Motors proclaimed its new-found romance with many forms of racing. Under the simple subhead "Rebel," AMC announced: "A new Rebel 'Funny Car' has been built (under our sponsorship) by Grant Industries of Los Angeles. This association was very successful last year, setting new ¼ mile track records of 8.11 seconds and 180.85 mph at Tampa. At the end of last season Hayden Proffitt had established six track records and one national speed record with the Rebel. Not bad for a first season."

The Rebel success in Grant-prepared clothing over three seasons led to the dramatic Rebel Machine prepared for the 1970 model year.

The 1970 Rebel Machine was a stunning vehicle that spoke performance just standing there. Its detriment was its weight—3,475 pounds. Its 390 engine was capable of 340 horsepower, the biggest engine in an AMC car to that time. It produced a hefty 430 lbs-ft. of torque as well.

The Machine had the Hurst-shifted four-speed and came with a 3.54 rear end and an optional 3.91 unit. In tests the Machine did a quarter mile in 14.4 seconds at 99 mph.

The first 1,000 built were painted in the memorable red, white and blue. Later cars came

While many Ramblers touted economy, the SC/Rambler version was all about performance.

with a choice of paint schemes. The Machine also carried a functional, vacuum-operated hood scoop.

The model sported a wide hood scoop, a stylish hood tach, and a body-length stripe. Over 2,300 were produced with the first thousand finished in white, with the body and hood stripes done in blue. The remainder of the Machines, though, could be

The slinky, macho Rebel Machine carried a 390-cid, 340-hp power plant that certainly looked like a drag racing candidate.

bought in a number of different colors, all coming with silver pin striping and a blacked-out hood.

The national advertising campaign pointed to The Machine being a performance machine. Statements like: "A 390 engine comes as standard equipment and develops a horsepower the equivalent of 340 horses all pulling in unison, which is no mean feat... To feed air to your engine...we have bolted on a ram-air hood scoop, and mounted a tach that's lighted and registers to 8,000 rpm." And on and on!

The Machine had all the indicators that it could have lived up to its name and image. And AMC latched onto the irreverent streak in the young at the time with its "Up with Rebel Machine" cartoon in advertising.

The Machine followed up on the performance direction that the SC/Rambler and the drag racing Rebel SST had promised. Yet reviewers, including *Hot Rod* magazine were disappointed in the rather plodding outcome of the Machine. It was produced for only the 1970 model year, though an option called the "Machine Package" was available on the 1971 Rebel and included a 330-hp, 401-cid V-8 engine.

Having the Machine trimmed down in weight and that engine tuned to greater performance would have appeared to make this the ideal lightweight drag car, but that just didn't happen.

The Winner—The AMX

What did happen was that AMC selected its pony car, the AMX, to serve as the basis for its lightweight competitor. After all, the Camaro, GTO and Mustang

Introducing the Rebel "Machine."

Standing before you is the car you've always wanted.

And, if you like everything about it, except for the paint job, which admittedly looks startling, you can order the car painted in the color of your choice.

You may be wondering why a company like American Motors would paint a car red, white and blue.

And that's what we keep asking ourselves: Why would a company like American Motors paint a car red, white and blue?

But we have nothing to be embarrassed about under the hood, which is all you should be concerned about.

The Machine has a 390 CID engine as standard equipment and develops a horsepower the equivalent of 340 horses all pulling in unison, which is no mean feat.

Next, and this will be particularly impressive to those people who have buried their heads in hot rod magazines since they were old enough to say "zoom . . . zoom . . . lookee it's a car," the Machine has a 4-speed all-synchromesh close-ratio transmission with special Hurst shift linkage and a 3.54:1 standard rear axle ratio (or an optional 3.91:1).

To feed air to your engine, once you buy the car, we have bolted on a ram-air hood scoop. And in the hood scoop, we mounted a tach that's lighted and registers 8000 rpm's.

Heavy-duty shocks and springs raise the rear end a bit and give the Machine, a raked,

just mowed the lawn look.

And our dual exhaust system uses special low back pressure mufflers and larger exhaust pipes.

We will make the description of the rest of the Machine's features mercifully short. Front and rear sway bars, high-back bucket seats, 15 inch tires with raised white letters, mag styled steel wheels, power disc brakes, and racing stripes that glow in the dark.

Incidentally, if you have delusions of entering the Daytona 500 with the Machine, or challenging people at random, the Machine is not that fast. You should know that.

For instance, it is not as fast on the getaway as a 427 Corvette, or a Hemi, but it is faster on the getaway than a Volkswagen, a slow freight train, and your old man's Cadillac.

In short, in order to fully make up your mind about the Machine, you will have to see it in person at your American Motors dealer.

And when you're introduced to it, a simple "How do you do?," "Nice meeting you," or something friendly like "How are your pipes?," will suffice.

Up with The Rebel Machine

For a set of four "Up with the Rebel Machine" decals send 25¢ and your name and address to: Machine Decal Offer, American Motors Sales Corporation, 14250 Plymouth Road, Detroit, Michigan 48232.

In an era when protests were quite common, AMC used the concept in the slogan "Up with the Rebel Machine."

were making noises during the later years of the 1960s. The AMC version would become known as the SS/AMX.

The corporate charge that spurred the AMX was a sea change for AMC, a company that saw the

The Rebel Machine was inspired by the Grant Pistons/ AMC "Machine" Rebel SST dragster.

The AMX prototype was popular and marked a new era for American Motors Corporation.

handwriting on the wall by 1966 and '67 when its "Sensible Spectacular" auto campaign was losing millions of dollars. AMC said it was ready to "… capture the younger generation's imagination and down payment."

An early prototype appeared at the 1966 Society of Automotive Engineers convention, a shell of a car with a quirky rumble seat under a glass hatch. Feedback was positive.

Several prototypes were sent out on a summer tour to gain public opinion. The cars had names like Vixen and Cavalier. The car that was chosen from the various designs was the Javelin. It met AMC's goals of being different and having charisma and appeal.

The Javelin was a four-seat car but AMC executives also wanted to introduce an even sportier two-seat version. Back in design, the approved Javelin wheelbase was shortened by a foot and that

gave the car its own special appearance when the Javelin hood, doors, windshield, rear deck, bumpers and more were retained. The name came from the program—American Motors Experimental, or AMX.

Car Life reported in their March 1968 review of the new AMX that AMC leaders were comparing the AMX to an American icon.

"American Motors executives are emphatic about the relationship of the AMX to Chevrolet's Corvette," said the magazine. "What is the AMX? It's a car to show the world that American Motors is in the high-performance market."

While the four-seat Javelin was targeted as a pony car, the AMX came with a racing swagger, with its only engine choices being the AMX 390-cid, 315-hp V-8 that produced 425 lbs.-ft. of torque at 3,200 rpm. With heavy duty suspension and traction bars available, the AMX was a potent package that sold 67,000 copies its first year or

The early AMC focus was on the four-place Javelin.

A 1970 press photo of the AMC Javelin.

The AMX was introduced in 1968 as a two-seat car with a powerful engine.

15,000 more than the Javelin.

Car Life noted that a veteran AMC engineer seemed shocked when he witnessed a rubber burning and fire-breathing test of the AMX mumbling the car wasn't intended for that kind of treatment.

"The AMX is not only intended for this kind of driving," said *Car Life,* "it is a great tool for it."

AMC quickly formed a racing team and introduced the Javelin—the four-seat AMC car and the AMX into various drag racing and Trans Am racing competitions. Early tests showed the Super Stock AMX could hit speeds of up to 125 mph in the quarter mile and with more preparation, it was even a better performer.

The AMX turned out to be one hot machine with a capability of 10.13 seconds and 131 mph in the quarter. It was good, very good. So good in fact, that it kept being reclassified when it kept whipping up on each higher class.

It goes without saying that American Motors was starting very late with its Lightweight, where the Big Three had been doing it since the early 1960s. But the company was serious about the reported 52 SS/AMX models that were constructed.

In the March 1968 issue of *Motor Trend,* reviewer Bill Sanders wrote this about the AMX:

"It has approximately the same dimensions as the Corvette, a wheelbase of 97 inches, with front tread measuring 58.36 inches..."

"At the drag strip...the AMX owner shouldn't develop any inferiority syndromes. Short wheelbase

Another image of the 1968 AMX taken on a snowy day.

and big engine in the AMX make a world of difference in all performance characteristics."

AMC styling chief Dick Teague called the AMX "... a hairy little brother to the Javelin."

No wonder the AMX was the leader in AMC's lightweight endeavors!

In a 1968 ad called "American Motors Modified" the Kenosha car-builders proclaimed their emphasis on racing and the AMX.

"Even before we officially introduced the AMX, it broke 90 Class C records (with a modification of the 290 engine bored out to 304 cid). Naturally, we're encouraged and plan to enter the AMX in other racing events in the near future."

The black rims gave a small indication that racing was the business here, no fancy chrome rally wheels here. Their purpose was to help lighten the front end so it could be lifted during launch from the starting line. On some cars, the factory also radiused the rear wheel wells before released to the owners.

The company wanted the cars to be as successful as possible. To that end, there were performance enhancement bulletins that were sent out from the company. There were updates on the rules governing the cars to make sure the teams knew about them.

With what came with the SS/AMX, the race team could hit the track almost immediately. First, there was that potent 390 power plant that punched out a factory-reported 405 horsepower. Recall that the competition was running either 426 or 427 cubic inch engines. The rear end ratio was geared at a 4.44 ratio.

The cars were then shipped to Hurst where they received a major workover. In the fall of 1969, the standard AMXs were pulled from the assembly line and shipped to the Hurst facility in California. They were identical Frost White 390-powered, four-speed models. When Hurst completed its modification job, the AMXs would end up being far different beasts.

First, the engine was pulled and received forged JE Pistons, Crane-modified cylinder heads, cross ram intake, Mallory dual point distributor with mechanical tach drive, and clear-flowing Doug Thorley exhaust headers.

Cool air was then funneled into the dual carbs from the functional hood scoop. When NHRA looked at the factory's 340 horsepower quote, they raised it to a more realistic 420.

Hurst then massaged the Borg Warner T-10, installing a 2.64-1 low gear ratio. The tranny was joined up with a sturdy bell housing. It was shifted with a Hurst Super Shifter unit. The factory limited-slip rear end was left in place.

Hurst then moved to the suspension system and installed single-piece axles along with replacing the factory springs and shocks with pure racing equipment. The front sway bar was left off, not needed, and, of course, its omission saved weight. The car wasn't intended for making any turns at high speeds. Reportedly, Hurst also relocated the right-rear spring hanger.

There were lots of other factory parts that were deleted which produced considerable lightening. They included items such as the hood latches that were not needed as hood pins were now in place. Grille supports, front fender brackets, along with springs and hinges were also omitted. And would you believe, one of the horns was even left off?

REBEL:
The Pioneer Lightweights

In the 1957 model year, American Motors Corporation was in transition, preparing to lead the way to the economy car trend of the late 1950s. It was preparing to phase out its full-size Nash Ambassador and Hudson car lines and was ready to lead the way to economy with its mid-sized Rambler, restyled in 1956 and available in both small six and V-8 editions.

Yet one Nash Rambler ran against the conforming culture of the decade and even against its own corporate direction. Introduced on Dec. 4, 1956, and displayed at the New York National Auto Show that month, heads turned in performance circles. The car was a four-door hardtop version of the Rambler called the Rebel and it was worthy of that name.

Silver with gold anodized trim on the outside and produced only in a four-door hardtop with a dapper continental kit in back, it seemed like another family sedan. Yet it was something else under the hood and underneath its chassis.

The Rebel used the 327-cid, 255-hp Ambassador V-8 complete with its four-barrel Carter WCFB carburetor setup. With a stronger cam, beefed-up drive train, stiffer springs, better brakes and Gabriel adjustable shocks, the Rebel was quite strong in its stance.

The Rebel made a statement for American Motors. It was as if to say that AMC could join the fray if it chose to do so, but it was following the lead of then AMC president George Romney who encouraged automakers to cut back on factory-sponsored racing.

The 3,350-pound Rebel package also predicted what could happen in the decade to come when a large V-8 was stuffed into a mid-size car. AMC limited Rebel production to just 1,500 copies.

Reportedly, the Rebel would have had 288 horses had AMC not had troubles with the Bendix "Electrojector" electronic fuel injection system. But the 255 carbureted horses provided worked well. In April 1957, *Motor Trend* tested the Rebel and found the car was second only to the fuel-injected Corvette V-8 in runs on Daytona Beach in Florida.

The Rebel's spare tire and back end was front and center on the April 1957 cover of *Motor Trend* and inside, Joe H. Wherry conducted a "Drivescription" of the car.

"…the compression ratio is a now more or less high 9.5 to 1," wrote Wherry. "With the conventional four-barrel carburetor the output is 255 horses at 4,700 rpm and torque is 345 pounds-feet at 2600."

"A Rambler it is in essence," Wherry continued, "but the Rebel represents a counter-revolutionary move on the part of AMC—they're out to prove they can make 'em go fast as well as cheaply."

Buyers of the limited production Rebel could accept the standard three-speed manual transmission or order the optional "Flashaway" Hydra-Matic gearbox.

Hot Rod magazine tested the Rebel with Hydra-Matic and sped to a 9.4-second, 0-to-60 time and also reported an 8-second time in a manual transmission version. *Motor Trend* recorded a 7.5-second time in its 0-to-60 acceleration test with the Rebel.

"It's unlike any other car made in this land," observed *Motor Trend* writer Wherry. "…it has the quality and performance of many more costly cars, as much interior space as many and a personality all its own."

The Rebel had a short run in 1957 due to tight production budgets and a limited number of available dealers. AMC's advertising coffers weren't deep enough to compete with the deep-pocket advertising programs of the Big Three late in the 1957 model year. But the Rebel predicted something else for the North American car buying public.

In just seven years, Pontiac would introduce the powerful GTO and lead the charge to mid-size muscle cars. The Rambler Rebel pioneered the concept and certainly had all the earmarks of a factory-produced lightweight, several years prior to the use of the term.

Legendary Lightweight: The 1957 Rambler Rebel	
Engine:	OHV Rebel V-8
Displacement:	327 cid with 255 hp @ 4,700 rpm
Carburetion:	Carter WCBF four-barrel
Bore and stroke:	4 x 3 ¼ inches
Compression:	9.0:1
Weight:	3,353 lbs.
Notes:	Five bearings with solid valve lifters
Factory price:	$2,786

Veteran Hayden Proffitt drove these Rebel SSTs from 1967-69.

Right off the bat, the model didn't have any rocker panel moldings. Guess it goes without saying that there was also the long-standing radio and heater deletes.

But there were more items that were in the delete category, including the likes of carpet padding, sound deadening, and other accessory items.

Hurst also had to open up the rear wheel wells in order to accept the 10-inch racing slicks. There was even some "assembly required" aspect of the model as the finish of the hood scoop openings, rear wheel cutouts and carpet were left to the responsibility of the race team to complete to their likes.

For the time period, the SS/AMX cost the buyer a ton, actually about twice the price of the SC/Rambler and about $1,600 more than The Machine. But considering the amount of modification work that had been done by Hurst, it was still a bargain!

The cars were delivered with the headers, velocity stacks, shifter T-handles and decals, all in the trunk. The battery was already installed in that location.

Like all the other lightweight drag cars from the other manufacturers, there was a special notice given with purchase. AMC worded it as follows:

"This car is equipped with a specially modified 390 cu. in. engine (and other special equipment). This car is intended for use in supervised acceleration trials and is not intended for highway or general passenger car use. Accordingly, the vehicle is sold 'AS IS' and the 12 month or 12,000 mile vehicle warranty coverage and 5 year or 50,000 mile power train warranty coverage does not apply."

There certainly didn't need to be any further explanation that you were purchasing a pure-bred race machine! An interesting note was that these cars were delivered with mufflers in place, which

Wow, dad's Rambler sure doesn't look like this!

"Bonzai" Bill Hayes also drove the Grant Pistons Rebel.

made them street legal with a little work.

Considering the fact that AMC would have hardly been considered a performance-oriented company, the mid-10 second performance that was immediately demonstrated surprised many.

But even so, the models were not immediately accepted and many of them were fielded by AMC dealerships.

The cars competed with both NHRA and AHRA. In the former, it was in the C Stock Class, while the

The Mr. Pickett Javelin was driven by Bob Pickett. Bob Plumer

latter group had them in its Super Stock Eliminator Class.

One driver who turned heads in her SS/AMX was Shirley Shahan. By the end of 1969, she'd taken AMC from barely a blip in drag racing circles to several new SS/D class records that put the cars from Kenosha in third place in NHRA standings for the year.

In a May 1969 poll, the AMX got more votes than many contemporary cars including the Triumph TR250, the Morgan Plus 8, the Lotus Europa and Elan, The MGB and MGC, among others.

The AMX Registry has identified 32 of the approximate 52 AMX/SS models as interest in these cars continues to grow through the years. Many of these cars have been restored to their original configurations, including duplicating their original paint schemes. A few still carry that early livery.

Two of the best known SS/AMX cars were purchased by the Wentworth and Irwin team through their dealership. One was modified as a wheel-standing vehicle while the other was campaigned as the "Little Bossa Nova 2." That latter car still remains today.

Some of the top SS/AMX drivers included the likes of Lou Downing in the "Pete's Patriot," Gary Stowe, Shirley Shahan in the "Drag-On-Lady," and Joe Thomas in the "AMXpress."

One of the best examples of the SS/AMX breed is the one owned by Rick and Paulette Riley of Middletown, Ohio. This car was number 18 of those built and one of those that received the red, white, and blue paint scheme, and that's the color combination that it continues to carry today.

It had a significant history in that it won the AHRA Summer Nationals and was runner-up in Super Stock Eliminator with a world record of 11.08 at 127.11 miles per hour. The Rileys restored the car and it has had a huge number of honors at national car shows. Between 1991 and 1995, the car was on display at the Otis Chandler Vintage Museum of Transportation in Oxnard, California.

Rick laughed when he explained that there was only .7 miles on the odometer cable when it was cut. It's still that way today. Rick also indicated, "I had the engine dynoed and it was close to 600 horsepower."

AMC connoisseur George Gudat is one of the most enthusiastic and knowledgeable of those cars. "It's number 36 of the cars built and was driven by Kim Nagel, mostly in local competition in Missouri, Kansas, and Oklahoma. Its best effort was an 11-second, 118 mile-per-hour run. It also still has its original paint."

The Drag-On-Lady AMX driven by Shirley Shahan.

Bob Plumer

Gudat also provided an interesting tidbit of information with the fact that only five-or-so of these cars competed nationally.

How about this AMX/SS that carries the original weathered words of "Cotton Candy!" The car, which was the 11th built, is owned by Dave Dante and was initially campaigned locally by one Darrell Beswdeck into the late 1970s. Then it sat for many years before Dante made the purchase. Amazingly, the car still carries its original drive train!

One of the best known of these AMC Super Stockers is the number 39 car owned by Mike Pearce. The "Pete's Patriot" was originally owned by Pete Peterson who was an AMC dealer. Pearce restored the car to amazing accuracy.

Pearce explained that the car was the NHRA Division V Champion in 1969. "It was also the only one of these cars that held a national record at the time," Mike explained.

The famous car was in a woeful condition when the purchase was made. "I worked with original driver Lou Downing who pointed out the little things that made me know that I had the real car.

The most interesting fact was that there was a broken coil in the seat that punched him in the back when he was on a hard run. Hey, it's still there!"

There was even an attempt to have the SS cars continue to compete in the 1970 season. AMC even went to the trouble to offer a kit to make the conversion, but the NHRA rules wouldn't allow it. But a number of these cars reportedly continued to compete in the 1969 configuration.

Rick Gunderson owns one of those cars that had the 1970 conversion, and it shows that there were quite a few changes made to the '60 model. Gunderson explained that his car carries those '70 additions, including a new hood, front bumper, grille, dash, seats, and taillight panels. "This car, by the way, did run nationally when it carried the name of 'Wicked and Nasty.'"

The AMX and its sibling, the Javelin, were a runaway success for AMC in 1968 selling 52,000 Javelins and 67,000 versions of the AMX.

"With the AMX," wrote automotive historian Robert Ackerman in a 1981 *Automobile Quarterly* retrospective, "American Motors leap-frogged over the competition, creating, not only an effective image changer, but one which also catered to a totally different slice of the market."

1969 Hurst AMX SS Specifications	
Engine:	AMC 390 V-8
Carburetion:	Holley dual 615-cfm, four barrels
Displacement:	390-cid
Horsepower:	340 hp (420 hp per NHRA specs)
Bore and stroke:	4.165 x 3.574 inches
Torque:	420 lbs.-ft. @ 3,400 rpm
Transmission:	Borg-Warner T-10 four speed
Axle:	Dana 20 Twin-Grip 4.44:1
Weight:	3,050 lbs.
Price:	$5,994
Best time:	9.53 seconds @ 140 mph

Note: The AMX SS used a forged steel crankshaft and connecting rods with the stock AMC hydraulic camshaft. Monroe drag-style shocks were used front and back. The car came with stamped steel wheels.

Source: April/May 1996 *Muscle Car Review*

1967 Rambler Rebel SST

Although it didn't get the publicity of the later SS/AMX, the Rambler Rebel SST was a highly-successful lightweight machine. It all came about in early 1967 when Grant Industries accepted a contract from American Motors to build a lightweight Rambler Rebel-based funny car-style vehicle.

The factory 343-cid engine was used as a starting point for the SST power plant. The engine was bored out to 443 cubic inches, hooked to a supercharger and used nitro fuel. The result was 1,200 horsepower at 9,000 rpm! Proffitt explained that it was a one-off machine.

The amazing aspect of the story was that Chevrolet driver, and NHRA superstar, Hayden Proffitt came on board to wheel the AMC machine. Proffitt showed the lightweight fiberglass-bodied machine really had what it took turning a best of 172 mph/8.5 second clocking at the '67 NHRA nationals.

"It was a three-year factory contract with the Rebel SST program, and I continued to drive the model through the 1968 and 1969 seasons," Hayden explained. It should be noted that AMC was the final of four brands of lightweight machines Proffitt drove in his career, the only driver that could make that statement.

SHIRLEY SHAHAN:
The Famed Drag-On-Lady

For many years, driving a Chevrolet, a Plymouth, a Dodge Dart or an AMX, Gremlin or Hornet, Shirley Shahan was the pretty wife whose job outside the home was drag racing. Yet she surpassed that image to become one of drag racing's legendary drivers, regardless of gender.

Shirley began going to races in the mid 1950s because her husband, H. L., was involved as a driver in gas coupes, super stocks and dragsters as well as a mechanic and racing boat driver.

"It was either sit home or go with him," she told *Auto Topics* in December 1965. "So I went with him and soon became interested in the sport and learned to drive."

A mother of three, Shirley Shahan was a consistent winner on the drag strip.

"When we won stock class" she recalled at a recent NHRA California Hot Rod Reunion, "our prize was two cases of beer, two T-shirts and a wall plaque."

Shirley began her racing career in the 1950s. H. L. prepared their cars and Shirley's driving skills took them to the drag strips for competition.

In 1958, she entered 50 drag races and won them all. She drove an H.L.-tuned 1958 Chevy to a win in Super Stock at the first March Meet at Bakersfield, California, in 1959. Shirley had a lot of personal pride in her efforts.

"Drag racing to me is more than just fast time," she said in 1965. "It's making a name for yourself and personal recognition that really counts."

"Not too many people recall this," she said in a 1967 article, "but I drove a gas rail to speeds of 160 mph back as far as the early 1960s. The engine was a blown Cadillac at first. We changed to a Chevy later in the life of the car."

"You don't make many mistakes driving a car like this," she added. "It's no Sunday drive making a run in a stock bodied fueler."

By 1965, the Shahans were ready to take on a higher rung of drag racing competition and, with some Chrysler

backing, the Shahans bought a new Plymouth Super Stock. Reportedly, a Chrysler public relations professional coined the name that would always be with her, the "Drag-On-Lady."

Shirley also got more involved in the business end of the cars in the 1960s when she and H.L. began driving the Plymouth according to her husband.

"One night I came home from work and she had the whole Hemi torn down in the middle of the garage," recalled H. L.

In 1966, she became the first woman to win the Stock Eliminator championship at that year's Winternationals. The Shahans drove their Plymouth and later a Hemi Dodge Dart over four seasons winning several Super Stock crowns and also some fuel injected match races.

"It really doesn't matter what type fuel is being used if the total capability of the car places it in a high speed situation," she told *Hot Rod* writer Jim McFarland in 1967.

She also mentioned one the joys of drag racing in a mid-'60s profile.

"When a guy looks over my way and says 'That's all I have to beat?' and we run and I *beat* him! That's a type of satisfaction only a woman can understand."

At the end of the AMC experience, Proffitt's career with those cars basically ended. "The factory support went away and it just got too expensive to continue," he explained.

In addition, there was a new national record for one-eighth mile tracks. The Rebel SST also set track records at a number of tracks including a best of 180.85 mph in 8.11 seconds at the Tampa, Florida, Dragway. The machine was used as a great advertising tool as the car put on demonstrations across the national with driver

Bill Hayes behind the wheel. It was advertised that Hayes was looking for a 200-mph run, but it is unknown whether he ever accomplished that goal.

The 1968/1969 XP Package

It was called the XP package, an aftermarket modification from one Darrell Droke, which had definite Super Stock drag implications. The package was compatible with the 1968 and '69 Javelins and AMXs. The XP pieces consisted of a

As the attention of American Motors Corporation was focused on jump-starting their image, especially in Trans Am and drag racing circles, the Kenosha crowd was looking for good drivers. Hayden Proffitt had already made some rumblings in 1968 with the Grant Piston Rings/Rebel SST car.

As the 1969 season approached, Shirley and her husband, H. L., were approached by AMC to drive one of their new AMX cars, a 97-inch wheelbase rocket when prepared to drag racing standards. It was a step forward in Shirley's career.

The drag racing version of the AMX was prepared by Hurst and at 3,050 pounds it came with Doug's headers, an Edelbrock manifold, a healthy 12.3:1 compression ratio and a 4.44 rear end.

Shirley would set D/Super Stock records in 1969 with her AMX, then go on to set new records driving in the 1970 season.

In an era when women were hitting their stride in their quest for equality, Shirley Shahan had made her reputation keeping up—and beating—the best male drag racers of the era.

Hot Rod magazine's Steve Kelly put it this way in the December 1971 issue, reflecting the idea that some were catching up to the concept that women could be on such an equal setting.

"The likable Mrs. Shahan hasn't been spending much time at home, nor has she been taking very long to

Shirley Shahan and her AMX were featured in a 1969 AMC publication.

traverse the 1820. No doubt a large number of her drag racing fans would prefer that she stay home with the laundry and cleaning, but chances of her trading a gear-shift for a vacuum cleaner are remote."

A mother of three, Shirley was a records control clerk at a Southern California gas company. She also was an ardent softball player in addition to her drag racing career. Shirley was ahead of her time, pioneering drag racing success with other women of her generation including Shirley Muldowney, Paula Murphy, Judy Lilly, Donna Ireland and Robin Leighton.

"I love drag racing," Shahan said as she was honored in recent years at an NHRA reunion.

Like her contemporaries Shirley Shahan blew away the stereotypes and blasted through the competition in her years of drag racing.

While she had attained a lot of success driving Plymouths, Dodges and other rides earlier in her career, she became arguably the most famous quarter mile driver for American Motors piloting AMX, Gremlin and Hornet drag racers over the years.

Shirley Shahan became a legend behind the wheel of lightweight drag racing cars. Emphasize the "drag-on" in her nickname and think of her as the lady who often finished in first place, ahead of all the boys who challenged her at the line.

lightweight fiberglass hood, fiberglass rear deck and optional functional hood scoop, hood tach, matching fender end caps, and a wrap-around spoiler. Finally, there were a number of appearance items including Cragar wheels, a wood-rimmed Grant steering wheel, and XP identifying emblems. An optional roll bar and unspecified under-hood refinements made this into a nifty low-cost drag machine. There was also some involvement from Super Stock driver Ron Root who had made some suggestions on the package.

In its November 1968 issue, *Hot Rod* magazine tested an XP-equipped Javelin with an automatic transmission and street tires. It turned an impressive 14.30-second quarter-mile dash.

A few American Motors dealers bought the package that generated some interest. Unfortunately, neither XP-equipped AMXs or Javelins never made it to NHRA, but the potential was certainly there for them to have done so.

Chapter 2

CHEVROLET
LIGHTWEIGHTS

Chevy was one of two GM brands that played the Lightweight game. From a factory point-of-view, the models that played the game were the Biscayne, Bel-Air and Impala with the 409 engine types. As time went on the, Camaro, Chevelle, Corvair, Chevy II/Nova and Vega all would contribute to lightweight lore.

1961 Super Stockers

Early in the 1960s, there was an increasing interest in what would evolve as the Super Stock Division with NHRA.

Full-body Chevys were active competitors in that competition with '60 and '61 Chevys showing outstanding performance.

Initially, these cars were using the 348-cubic inch tri-power engines that were capable of about 340 horsepower. In some of these long-ago events, those supposedly non-lightweight Chevys were turning outstanding quarter-mile times.

Elwin Westbrook, a mechanic at Performance Associates, drove his 1960 Chevy at a record speed of 100.02 mph in 14.03 seconds. Later, Bruce Morgan set new records of 104.40 mph with a 14.04-second clocking.

This historic shot shows Don Nicholson's Chevrolet (right) versus an early Ramcharger Dodge.

Bob Plumer

"Jungle Jim" Liberman was famous for various Chevrolets, like this Chevy II.

Bob Plumer

But it had become evident that the 348 just wasn't going to get it done against the potent competition. That's when Chevy released the engine that would have 61 more cubic inches than the 348. It would be instantly successful and in the years to come, even legendary.

There were similarities between the 348 and the 409, but the new power plant was not just a bored-out version of the 348. The tolerances on the 348 were just too close to allow any boring out.

It was necessary to design a completely new block. And in addition to the increased bore on the new block, there was also a slight increase in stroke to acquire the additional displacement.

The new engine's characteristics sounded like they were pure-race inspired with forged pistons and larger intake and exhaust valves, and a single Carter four-barrel carb. There was also a lightweight aluminum intake manifold. With an impressive 11.25-1 compression ratio, the factory horsepower was

announced as 360. Many figured that number could well have been 20-30 horsepower understated with its high-performance components.

The new power plant quickly proved that it had what it took as "Dyno Don" Nicholson became the terror of the drag strips in his Chevy 409. *Super Stock* magazine's Mike Doherty wrote about

Bob Plumer

The late "Dyno Don" Nicholson drove this 1961 Chevrolet to fame.

Chevrolet made an impact in drag racing with this beautiful factory-built Impala with a 409.

Many saw the back end of the 1962 Zintmaster Chevrolet on drag strips.

The 1962 Chevy lightweight was "Plain Jane" at best with the deletion of the radio, heater and other interior amenities.

Two giant four-barrel carburetors were used on the performance version of the 409 engine. That resulted in an amazing 409 horsepower.

To maintain the Chevrolet look, the trim and emblems were usually retained on these cars.

Looking at this Chevrolet 409 V-8 air cleaner, it's hard to believe that two large four-barrels are nestled beneath it.

Nicholson's success with the engine in a 1968 article:

"[Nicholson] rang up 13.19-second, 109.48 mph times in trials, destroying the confidence of the name Ford and Pontiac pilots that intended to mow down the 348 Chevrolets at long last. They…watched Nicholson high-rev through to the class final against Frank Sanders in the other 409 released for the meet!"

And writer Doherty described the Impala "bubble top" two-door hardtop driven by Nicholson.

"The powerhouse Chevy carried a conservative power rating of 360 hp at 5800 rpm, with 409 lbs.-ft. of torque at 3600. Only one Carter four-barrel, but healthy 11.25-1 compression and a displacement advantage of 20 cubes on the competition."

Nicholson took the '61 Winternationals in Top Stock while Frank Sanders took Super Stock, both in 409 Impalas, and both in the mid-13 second category. Nicholson would follow with another Top Stock success at the '61 Nationals. A certain amount of modification was allowed which included some engine lightening.

In August of 1961, Chevrolet introduced a retooled drag package with dual four-barrel carbs, heads with bigger ports, large 2.19-inch intake valves and a new cam for drag racing. The horses were boosted to 409 as well, predicting the 1962 engine. The hotter 409 breathed air through a new hood scoop. Nicholson went on to beat Al Eckstrand's Ramcharger Dodge in a memorable two-out-of-three run competition with this factory updated Chevy 409.

1962 Chevy Lightweights

Things changed big time in 1962 with the introduction of a greatly-revised 409, now with the production version of revisions tested at the drag strips late in 1961. The 409 was perked at an 11.5-1 compression ratio. With revised 409 cam profiles, and a dual-quad carburetion set-up resting on an aluminum intake manifold, the new engine also had a small weight loss. The carbs were a pair of the highly efficient Carter AFB version.

In addition, there were both new valves and valve springs. For better exhaust flow, the exhaust manifolds were redesigned, all resulting in a one-horsepower per cubic-inch 409 horsepower rating. That performance accomplishment was certainly a great advertising ploy for the company. There was also a 389 single-carb version of the killer mill. The Chevy Impala SS was the model of choice for the introduction of the potent new 409.

Chevy realized performance on the drag strip was worth gold in national advertising and wanted to be competitive. In July 1962, Chevy built about 25 aluminum front-end models to determine the effect the lightweight metal would have on the production process. The models so endowed included both Chevrolet Biscaynes and the upscale Impala SS 409s.

The Factory Lightweight cars were built specifically for professional race teams and were not available to the general public. However, there was a limited amount of the aluminum pieces that could be bought over the Chevy parts counters.

On the competition trail, things kept getting better with NHRA suddenly allowing use of the so-called "409 Service Package" that contained a number of performance goodies, including a high-lift cam, stronger pistons, a performance intake manifold, and a free-flowing exhaust system. Also, the interiors certainly didn't carry any additional weight with radio- and heater- delete options.

Above: *The Impala model was selected for the lightweight application in 1962 and 1963.*

Below: *Jim MacKenzie's accurate replica of Dave Strickler's 1962 Bel Air lightweight. MacKenzie won the 2003 NMCA championship with the car.*

Here is a period shot of Dave Strickler's 1963 Z 11 Impala on its flatbed Chevy hauler. Bob Plumer

"Fast Eddie" Schartman drove this 1963 Chevrolet Z 11 sponsored by Jack Shaw Chevrolet.
Bob Plumer

In addition, there was a four-speed manual transmission, metallic brakes, and Positraction rear end. A number of teams also slightly bored the blocks and installed aftermarket headers to reduce back pressure, among other Chevrolet factory-approved modifications to the cars.

The performance was certainly in place, so it was then decided that the use of aluminum was the best way to minimally reduce the significant weight of the cars. It would be used only in the front end of the cars.

An excellent example was the Zintsmaster Chevrolet-sponsored Impala that has been accurately restored by Indiana Chevy dealer Sam Pierce.

The example is correct in every aspect and carries the 409-cid, 409-hp power plant. The power train consists of the original four-speed transmission. Pierce also explained,

"I have five original tires, including the last set of M&H Racemasters that were used on the car. It also has the original metallic brakes, along with all the aluminum front end components."

He added that very little restoration was required to bring the car to the condition shown here.

It was very competitive. In October of 1962, at the Muncie, Indiana, Dragway, this Chevrolet took the Stock Eliminator title beating out the top competition of Jim Wangers in a Royal Pontiac Super Stock Pontiac. The car also made it into the final rounds of the '62 Nationals.

Estimates were that the metal substitution resulted in the saving of about 120-to-130 pounds when compared with the steel components. The "all-aluminum front end" nomenclature actually included the fenders, inner fender panels, and hood being fabricated in the light metal.

And you have to believe, these panels were extremely light and even flimsy, so much that many teams had signs on them indicating "Don't touch, aluminum!" The hoods would actually twist when raised. Needless to say, there were other lightening modifications made by the teams to bring the weight of the cars down even more.

NHRA had to make a decision where the Lightweight Chevys would run, and it was decided that the so-called Factory Experimental A/FX Class would be it. The competition was menacing with the Max Wedge Dodges and 421 Pontiac Tempests.

It was nearly a Pontiac sweep at the '62 Internationals, three out of four classes, but Nicholson did get the Top Stock Class in a 1962 409 Impala, turning an impressive 12.63-second run.

At the 1962 Nationals, the 409s garnered both Super Stock (with Dave Strickler at the wheel) and ex-Pontiac driver Hayden Proffitt in Top Stock Eliminator. Proffitt indicated that the event was one of the highlights of his illustrious career as he took the win over one of the vaunted Dodge Ramcharger machines.

1963 Z-11 Lightweights

The corporate claims of "We Don't Race" didn't seem to get down to the design engineers who were going full-bore for performance on the national drag strips. Chevy was right in there with a new Z-11 nametag. By the way, that "Z" prefix identified a model that carried special equipment, which in this case was high-performance equipment.

The Z-11 was just about the best there was as it addressed both the engine compartment with increased power, but there was also considerable lightening done.

Today, these cars are extremely rare with only a handful of the original 55 to 57 that were produced that model year. The Z-11 Impalas were produced in

only that single 1963 model year, with 25 released on the first of December 1962, followed by another 25 on New Year's Day. The final cars would be released later in 1963. The cars had a shipping weight of about 3,245 pounds. The limited number produced was because shortly afterward, all assembly of them was shut off due to the no-racing GM edict.

Six of the Z-11s went to the top teams like Butch Leal, Ronnie Sox, Don Nicholson, and Dave Strickler/Bill Jenkins. One of the lesser-known racers who got one was Malcolm Durham, who worked at D.C. Hicks Chevrolet in Washington, D.C. and who did his own engine work and car building.

Durham ran the car initially as an A/FX car, setting a class record. Later, it would run in the A/Modified Production Class and ran through the 1964 season before being sold to another driver. Then, after campaigning the car for a short period, it was set aside. Finally, collector Jerry Bryant would make the purchase and restore it to its initial "Strip Blazer" configuration.

The Z-11 immediately showed its excellence in the 1963 Winternationals when Frank Sanders took his Chevy to the Limited Production Class Championship. Also, in the A/FX Class, Z-11 driver Bill Shrewsberry took the title. Dave Strickler would repeat the A/FX accomplishment at the '63 Nationals.

The Z-11 nomenclature was officially identified as the $1,237 RPO "Special Performance Equipment Package" that included a special 427-cid, 430-hp engine, a four-speed transmission, a 4.11 Positraction rear end, vented drum brakes, numerous aluminum parts, and deletion of sound deadener materials.

Right off the bat, the Z-11 started off as a stock 1963 Impala two-door hardtop body. But there was aluminum galore with the front fenders, hood and

The 1966 Chevelle "funny car" of Bruce Larson was hand built and used considerable aluminum body panels. It used a number of big block, fuel-injected engines.
John Durand

hood scoop, splash pan, grille brackets, core support, gravel panel, fan shroud, water pump, front and rear bumper and mounting brackets. The lightness of the bumpers was sometimes demonstrated by them actually wrinkling up when a Z-11 was pouring on the coal. In addition, there were a number of deletes, including soundproofing material, insulation and the front sway bar.

Of course, the teams themselves also made modifications to the Z-11s when they got them. Noted on Don Nicholson's Z-11 was the removal of the headlight assembly on the outer lights, which in addition to lightening the car, also provided a path for cool outside air for engine cooling.

It has been reported that 18 1962 Impala drag cars built late in the year incorporated some of the lightweight Z-11 aluminum parts. Dave Strickler, in one of the cars that was modified for match racing, turned a 11.53-second, 123-mph run in his "Old Reliable" machine.

But as far as most Chevy experts are concerned, the heart and soul of the Z-11 package was that restless monster waiting under the hood. The engine was based somewhat on the previous 409 engine, but the displacement was now up to 427 cubic inches.

That figure was actually the result of a consultation with NASCAR and NHRA on what would be the maximum displacement for competition with either motorsports group. Recall that Ford also had its 427 engine, and there was Chrysler with its 426 Hemi power plant.

A Z-11 engine sidelight involved another Chevy race engine with the same displacement, the so-called "Mystery Engine" which was used with great success at the 1963 Daytona 500, winning both 100-mile qualifying races and setting a new track record. Much of the Z-11 technology was incorporated in that engine, but when the GM ban came, the Mystery Engine disappeared. However, in 1967, the 427 figures would appear again, and it was a direct descendent of the Mystery Motor.

Starting from the beginning, the blocks for the 409 and Z-11 engines were the same. But that's where the similarity ended, with the Z-11 being stroked up 18 cubic inches to the legendary 427 number.

Internal Z-11 parts were a whole new ballgame with new rods, crank, heads, and pistons. However, there were some similarities with the 409-cid, 425-hp engine with the dual-carb set-up. The factory-announced Z-11 horsepower was a conservative 430, but those in the know indicated that it was probably more in the 470-to-480 horsepower range.

One of the most-interesting Z-11 cars is that owned by Hank Gabbert, the former Jack May-owned car. Gabbert explained, "The car was built in December 1962 and was one of the first 25

Bruce Larson poses with some trophies in front of the 1967 version of his Chevelle.

Bob Plumer

constructed. [It] was driven by Larry Wilson and was race-prepared by Ronnie Sox of the famous Sox and Martin Race Team. It was sponsored by Sox Sinclair Service which was Ronnie's dad's business."

Hank indicated that all those people have been located and talked to about the car, and that they were all glad the car had been located and correctly restored.

Another Z-11 that is still around and in its original-style livery is the "Barber John" model that was sponsored by Smith Chevrolet of La Porte, Indiana. The car was on top during the 1964 through 1967 time period with "Barber John" Stepanek at the wheel. All he did was take NHRA titles in 1964, 1965, and 1967!

1964 and 1965 Chevelle and Chevy II Lightweights

Even though Chevy was out of racing, the remaining Z-11 engines most certainly were not. In 1964, a number of drivers removed their engines and placed them in different vehicles, with Chevelles and Chevy IIs being the most-likely recipients.

One such driver was Malcolm Durham who was one of the original recipients of the engine. His 1964 Chevelle was strictly a lightweight model geared for match racing. Durham used fiberglass to fabricate the front bumper, hood and front fenders. The inboard headlights were also eliminated for cooling purposes.

The 1969 Fred Gibb Chevrolet Camaro was driven by Dick Harrell.

Dick Harrell used such a machine in both 1964 and 1965 with his "Good Guys" Chevelle that came close to getting into the 10s. Harrell also had his lightweight "Retribution" Chevy II, also Z-11 powered. And Bill Thomas constructed a trio of lightweight Z-11 powered Chevy IIs. It should be noted that the Chevy IIs already had a built-in lightweight advantage being about four pounds lighter than the full-size Chevys.

One of the most-famous Chevy IIs was a homemade match-race car. The "Chevy 2 Much" was an altered wheelbase car that surprisingly didn't use lightweight materials in its body. Instead it kept the factory sheet metal. But it was lightweight in every other sense of the word, being completely gutted out and weighing a super-light 1,900 pounds!

The exciting Corvair of the Pisano Brothers in action.
Bob Plumer

Dick Harrell's Yenko Camaro in action.
Bob Plumer

The "Chevy II Much" was one of the first drag cars to use the new Chevy 396 porcupine-valve big block engine and it was fuel injected in this application.

The "Chevy II Much " was built and driven by Doug Thorley of the famous Doug's Headers Company. Today a replica of the real thing exists and it was constructed by Doug himself.

It is just one example of the popularity of the light Chevy IIs and Chevelles that were ideal choices for drag racing conversion.

Dick Harrell was a cover boy with his 1969 Fred Gibb Camaro.
Phil Hall Collection

1966 Chevy Lightweight Chevelles, Corvairs and Chevy IIs

But there was one other lightweight Chevy II-type that made headlines during the period. During 1966, it was possible to buy a Chevy II off the showroom floor with a ground-pounding L-79 350 horse 327-cubic inch flame-thrower. Combine that performance with a model that weighed just over 2,800 pounds and you had a factory-made drag machine, although the company probably didn't have that in mind at the time.

And an option possibility was the car could be ordered with the heater- and radio-deleted. Those deletions knocked off additional pounds. Talking about weight deletions, the lighter and carpet could also be deleted. Also, it was possible to order the M-21 Muncie tranny and a 12-bolt "posi" rear end.

In 1966, driver Duane Goodman liked what he saw with the Chevy II/L79 combination and his competitive career began that same year. Competing against the best there was, all he did was finish third at the 1966 NHRA Nationals. It was one of two Chevys that qualified for the Top Stock Eliminator— the other being Bill "Grumpy" Jenkins.

It's amazing when you think about it, that it was possible to make it to the big time, and be competitive, during your first year of competition. Recall, with GM out of the sponsoring picture, this was strictly a free-lance situation for these drivers.

The rules for the NHRA A/FX Class dictated that the wheels could not be altered in position more than two percent. But the fledgling Funny Car Class was offering more flexibility and as such a number of the top drivers went in that direction.

Such was the case of drag racing legend Bruce Larson, who in 1989 would be the NHRA Funny Car Champion. To that end, Larson constructed a wild lightweight machine based on a 1966 Chevelle SS. To accomplish significant body lightening, Larson had a boat manufacturer fabricate a complete set of fiberglass body panels.

In addition to a thousand horsepower injected nitro-burning power plant under the hood, there was considerable altering of the wheelbase, pulling the rear wheels forward an amazing 14 inches while the front wheels inched forward four inches.

The interior was gutted with just a single racing seat and re-fabricated from thin, light sheets of aluminum. Of course, no need for a radio, heater and other accessories. Further lightweight considerations were the complete deletion of the radiator that Larson didn't think was needed because of the short engine run. The headlights were eliminated and replaced by small Chevy hubcaps. The complete front end pivoted around the front of the car.

Even with the wild performance and lightweight implications of the car, it still carried a very stock look about it. Stock, that is, with the exception of the out-of-sight patriotic paint scheme. It was appropriately called the "USA-1," the name within the full length body strip. Also, a pair of stripes—one red and one blue cascaded over the length of the car.

The "USA-1" had a short but successful career with a best run of 8.78 seconds at about 160 miles per hour. Heady stuff for the time period, but about half of what the modern Funny Cars can do. Today, the car has been restored and is on display at the

A 1972 magazine cover shows that year's version of Grumpy Jenkins' Pro Stock Vega.
Phil Hall Collection

Don Garlits Museum in Ocala, Florida.

There was also the unlikely Corvair model that would find its way into national NHRA competition. The model that immediately comes to mind is the Corvair driven by legend Hayden Proffitt who recalled it with affection.

"It was really lightened up and only weighed about 2,400 pounds," Hayden recalled and added more details about the car. "It had an aluminum front end with lots of aluminum pieces. Then, it was powered by a big block supercharged engine that was burning 60 percent nitro. Over the year, I used engines that had 427, 454, and 488 cubic inches," he indicated.

Hayden laughed when he recalled, "We wanted to make the car even lighter so we cut off the top and

Grumpy Jenkins continued to win with this 1974 version of his Pro Stock Vega.

Phil Hall Collection

"STRIP BLAZER"
Malcolm Durham Blazed A Trail

The 1960s were a time for breaking barriers of race in American life. The Civil Rights crusade taught all Americans that segregation and prejudice were injustices past due repairing. During the decade, African-Americans began shattering old barriers they'd faced in American culture.

One of drag racing's first well known African-Americans was a Chevrolet driver born in Goldsboro, North Carolina.

Malcolm Durham began working on tractors growing up and took automotive technical classes after moving to Washington, D.C. Durham began racing a 1956 Chevy Bel Air with a 225-hp Corvette V-8 at such drag strips as Newton Grove and Aquasco Speedway. In 1958, he began competing and winning with a new 348-cid, 315-hp Chevy.

As a mechanic for D. C. Hicks Chevrolet in Washington, he drove and prepared a 1962 Chevy 409 with Z-11 heads and continued to win. He also built and maintained an A/ Production Corvette for sports car racing but drag racing was his preference.

He raced the first 1963 Chevy Z-11 available in the D.C. metropolitan area and used the name "Strip Blazer I."

He began to defeat bigger names like Dave Strickler and Grumpy Jenkins and soon earned a reputation as one of the top match racers on the East Coast.

When Chevrolet officially dropped out of drag racing the next year, Durham stuffed the 1963 Z-11's 427-cid engine into a new Chevelle and raced it as the "Strip Blazer II." It was a 3,200-lb. lightweight terror.

Durham's reputation climbed even higher in 1964 when he took on the legendary team of Ronnie Sox and Buddy Martin, A/Factory Experimental winners at that year's Winternationals. Durham and his Strip Blazer II Chevelle beat them at the 75-80 and Cecil County drag ways on consecutive nights, then continued to beat them three other times that year.

"It was my answer to Ford's 427 Thunderbolts," he said in an interview with Steve Waldron for the NHRA Top Drivers series. "We had the engine moved back eight inches from the stock location but we did it in a way that few people could detect."

He changed the Chevelle by adding new sheet metal plus outfitting it with injectors and nitro methane in 1965, then later raced a succession of Camaros. He broke the 200 mph barrier in 1969. His 1965 "Strip Blazer III" has been commemorated in miniature by Ertl.

Strip Blazers IV and V were configured and designed by Durham and ran with front-mounted 427-cid Chevy engines. By 1967, the Strip Blazer was running a best time in the 7.98 range, according to the December 1968 *Super Stock* magazine, and Durham was a success.

"When you're a drag racing superstar like me," he was quoted in 1968, "there's no such thing as hard work."

Durham later competed in Camaro- and Vega-based editions of the Strip Blazer.

"During the late 1960s, I averaged $800 per appearance," Durham recalled. "That made me one of the highest paid drivers in the business."

Durham's sons joined him in racing efforts. Bernard, like his father, is a drag racing driver while younger sons Raynard and Byron build racing engines.

"When I started, one or two guys could do it themselves," said Durham. "It's certainly not that way now. Drag racing has sure come a long way since my career began."

His racing success was recognized in 2001 as he was recognized as one of the Top 50 NHRA drag racers of all time. Today, Malcolm Durham can often be seen with other professionals of his time at vintage drag races. He often tells people he hasn't lost his desire for competition.

The "Strip Blazer" not only dazzled drag racing fans with his driving abilities, he blazed a trail for other African-Americans in the world of the quarter mile.

Malcom Durham switched to a Corvair with a front-mounted V-8 with the Strip Blazer IV. Bob Plumer

This shot shows both the Strip Blazer II Chevelle and Malcolm Durham's driving intensity.
Bob Plumer

1965 "Strip Blazer II" Specifications	
Engine:	427 Z-11 Chevrolet
Carburetion:	Dual Carter AFB four-barrel
Layout:	Front mounted, recessed 8 inches from stock
Horsepower:	450 stated, 600+ estimated
Compression:	13 to 1
Components:	'63 Pontiac driveshaft Oldsmobile rear axle '55 Buick coil springs Custom Forged-True pistons
Stock body:	1964 Chevelle Malibu two-door hardtop
Interior:	Stock plus Hurst shifter, custom lightweight bucket seats and Sun tach.
Wheels/tires:	Steel rims with 10-inch Racemaster tires, rear American mag wheels/standard tires
Notes:	Fiberglass front fenders, hood with working scoop, doors, trunk lid and bumpers by A & A Engineering. Plexiglass windows, windshield and rear window.
Weight:	3,200 lbs.

knocked off an additional 150 pounds. We ran the car in match races across the country and won about 60 of them. It was a great season!"

One of the greatest duals involved this car and the A/FX Comet of Don Nicholson at Irwindale Raceway, California. Both drivers mowed down the competition before meeting in the final.

Even though Hayden turned 158.17 mph, 18 mph faster than Nicholson, he had a half-second slower estimated time.

Malcolm Durham turned his attention to Corvairs with Strip Blazers IV and V in the mid 1960s. They were equipped with front-mounted 409-cid Chevy V-8s.

Another outstanding career in a Corvair was that of the Pisano Brothers Team. In 1969, with Frankie at the wheel, the machine blasted to a 7.435-second, 195.64-mph jaunt! The car featured a fiberglass flip-top body with an extended wheelbase.

The "Doug's Headers" Corvair, owned of course by Doug Thorley, was also another potent lightweight machine. The Corvair won the first NHRA Funny Car (that's what they called these altered cars) Eliminator race at Indy in 1967. At one time, this car was the fastest of the limited number of Corvairs with a 192.30-mph clocking.

THE CHEVY CONNECTION
to High Performance

There were many performance enhancements available for people who wanted to make their mild mannered cars into monsters in the 1960s. One combination that Chevy owners looked to was the Nickey Chevrolet and Bill Thomas connection.

Nickey, with the famous backward K, was located on Irving Park Road in Chicago, Illinois. Bill Thomas was based on East Julianna in Anaheim, California. Together, they covered the performance parts and speed equipment needs of Chevy-oriented customers across the country.

Nickey, a veteran high-volume Chevrolet dealer in the Chicago area, jumped into the performance auto world of the 1950s. The dealership owned and sponsored stock cars, drag racing cars, land speed record vehicles and sports cars.

One of their cars was called the "Purple People Eater," a racing Corvette. As drag racing gained in popularity, Nickey sponsored a Dick Harrell-driven funny car and a top-gas dragster piloted by Ron Colson.

When the Camaro was introduced in 1967, Nickey quickly produced a high performance version with a 427 Chevy engine.

Bill Thomas was the founder and leader of Bill Thomas Race Cars, a recognized West Coast preparer of cars, especially with Chevrolets. Chevy worked through Thomas, and later the combined Nickey-Thomas connection, to get results on the race tracks.

Chevrolet promoted an independent network to encourage racing through its Chevrolet Engineering Product Performance Group, often called "Chevrolet Racing Central." Thomas was respected in Chevy corporate circles because of his previous efforts in Chevy-based racing.

In 1966, Thomas prepared a Chevy II that was sponsored by Nickey and raced by Dick Harrell of Carlsbad, New Mexico. In addition to drag racing exposure, the cars became a prototype for the Nickey/Thomas mail order line. Many of the car's parts were available to the pubic.

The Nickey Chevrolet Chevy II in night action.

"Every major racing component in the car can be reproduced in detail for any requesting customer," wrote Larry Worthington in the June 1966 edition of *Car Life*.

"The mail order approach to weight reduction has shaved the weight of the Chevy II chassis 1,000 lbs. The most expensive box in the kit contains the engine, a 427-cid. Chevrolet built by Thomas to run on fuel blends of up to 70 percent nitro methane.

The article detailed all components used and available by mail order from Bill Thomas, a shopping list for drag racing performance.

In order to introduce the Camaro into competitive racing quickly and with a higher performance engine than was offered in 1967, the Nickey-Thomas connection was

The Nickey-Thomas partnership advertised aggressively during the late 1960s.

Bob Plumer

Writer Jim McFarland noted the Camaro's performance in testing at Irwindale Raceway.

"…the car was literally unbelievable in 3rd gear. Against the Ram-Air GTO our Eric Dahlquist was testing…we found the Camaro would open almost a car length of daylight. It was impressive. With open exhaust and the Casler slicks, the e.t. dropped to 12.50 and the speed bumped to 113."

The article went on to predict that with some minor preparations for racing, the Camaro could hit into the 11 range for an estimated time.

"Bill has everything you need for the package," the article promised. "You can literally build the car over the phone while you're ordering."

In December 1969, *Hot Rod* magazine showed what could happen with the Nickey-Thomas touch to a $400 used 1965 Chevelle 300 two-door sedan. The stock six-cylinder engine and three-speed transmission were replaced with the 427 V-8, helped with some additional engine mounts and some work on a clutch linkage. A four-speed transmission was added.

In order to handle the big block's hefty torque, the stock upper and lower control arms were replaced with a Mann Made traction bar assembly in back along with Delco heavy-duty shock absorbers and Air Lift bags with coil springs. Cure-Ride shocks were used in front. The Chevelle stock five-inch wheels and 7.35 x 14 tires were retained. A bigger radiator was used.

It was a very affordable change that made the Chevelle into a terror. And that's just what a lot of Chevy owners were looking for in the 1960s. Nickey Chevrolet and Bill Thomas Race Cars were only too willing to oblige.

Performance dealership Nickey Chevrolet was the sponsor of this Dick Harrell-driven Chevy II. John Durand

formed. They produced the ultimate in early Camaros, inserting the 427-cid, 425-hp engine into the cars and made Chevy's pony into a real racehorse.

Nickey-Thomas took SS 350 Camaros, often with Chevy's potent 396-cid engines, and replaced them with the heftier 427-cid versions. Modifications were made including the steering box and stock exhaust manifolds. In 1968, Nickey-Thomas

advertised their exclusive Camaro for $4,059.95.

A Nickey-Thomas prepared Camaro was profiled in the March 1968 issue of *Hot Rod.* Thomas was quoted about the engine switch.

"…we took this 425-horse 427 engine assembly, stuffed one of our 550 hydraulic cams into it, added a few handling pieces to the suspension and clamped on a set of tube headers and the results sorta tear your head off."

That record, though, would be blown away by the "Seaton's Super Shaker" Corvair of Terry Hedrick. The car started life as a 1966 Corvair alcohol-fueled car and later turned a 198.79-mile per hour blast.

COPO/Yenko/Gibbs/Harrell Novas

Chevy drag teams had long looked at the Chevy Nova as a possible drag machine. It was mainly for one reason—the Chevy II / Nova was much lighter than the other Chevy models of the 1960s era. Also, later versions of the model were equipped with the same 396 engines that were carried by the Chevelle. The most desirable of the big blocks was the L-78, which produced 375 horsepower.

When 50 of the L-78 models had been produced, Chevy requested NHRA establish a stock production class for the "hi-po" Novas. That's when the Fred Gibb Chevy dealership in La Harpe, Illinois, took over and did the modification of 50 cars at the dealership.

In addition to the lighter body, the COPO Novas also had a radio delete option. Officially, the Novas were given the COPO number of 9738. They were built to race and only carried a 90-day warranty. Bill Jenkins ran one of the cars during the 1978 season, and indicated that it was a time when Chevy was starting to come back.

At this time, 1968, Dick Harrell entered the scene and acquired some of the COPO Novas, making some conversions, including the installation of 427 engines.

"Grumpy's Toy"
Camaro from a
1970 Hot Rod
cover.

Some of the Harrell conversions also included lightweight fiberglass hoods.

Interestingly, some of these Harrell conversions were sold through authorized California Chevy dealerships!

Although it would have seemed like a logical maneuver in this performance era, there is no indication that the all-aluminum ZL-1 427 engine was ever installed in a COPO Nova. With the hundreds of pounds less the ZL-1 weighed, plus the lighter weight of the Nova, that would certainly have been the ultimate of lightweight factory machines.

The performance-oriented Yenko Chevy dealership in Cannonsburg, Pennsylvania had also ordered a number of the L-78 powered Novas and then replaced them with steel 427-cid, 435-horsepower L-72 Corvette engines. Those were the same engine the dealership would install in their Yenko Chevelles and Camaros.

The ZL-1 Camaro

It was the ultimate lightweight proposal. Take an already-light Camaro, and add a super-light aluminum engine. But not just any engine, the awesome ZL-1 427-cid, 430-hp power plant. That's exactly what happened in the late 1960s. The engine had already been proven in the Can-Am Racing Series.

The ZL-1 had pistons made by TRW and a healthy compression ratio—the factory said it was 12 to 1 but experts claim it was higher than 13 to 1. Many internal components came from the L-88 Corvette including their crankshafts and oil pan. The intake manifolds were rectangular while the exhaust ports were round. And new camshaft engineering was used for the ZL-1. A Holley four-barrel carburetor rated at 850 cfm topped off the amazing ZL-1 engine. Chevrolet also tacked on a cast iron water pump, cast iron exhaust manifolds and a special cold air induction system.

Super Stock and Drag Illustrated magazine tested a ZL-1 Camaro from Gibb Chevrolet for its May 1969 issue. The car was equipped with a Turbo Hydra-Matic transmission plus a standard 4.10 to one axle ratio. It came with a Holley vacuum 800-cfm carburetor that was replaced with the appropriate 850-cfm version.

Reportedly, Dick Harrell took the wheel and noted incredible wheel spin. He reached a top speed of 122.15 mph and a best time of 11.64 seconds after several runs and such tinkering as lashing the valves, disconnecting the headers and reducing air volume in the drag slicks. Later, another test was done on a four-speed version that ran a best time of 11.50 seconds.

But in order to be eligible for NHRA drag competition, it was necessary to build at least 50 of the number. No problem, as 69 were constructed, which made the model eligible to run in A Stock/Automatic and A Stock/Manual Classes.

Of the 50 ordered by Gibb Chevrolet, 30 were sold by Gibb but 20 were redistributed by Chevrolet to dealers in the U.S. and Canada. Chevrolet tacked on charges that boosted the ZL-1's price into the $7,500 range—at a time when a Camaro V-8 was less than $2,800.

The cars would later run in the new Pro Stock Class with the likes of Bill "Grumpy" Jenkins, Mike Fons, and others behind the wheel. These cars were capable of sub-10-second, 140-mph performance. The success of the ZL-1s was so significant that some drivers actually built homemade versions, dropping ZL-1 engines into existing Camaros. Jenkins reportedly put a personal ZL-1 engine into a 1967 Camaro!

Like the COPO Novas, Gibb Chevrolet was again involved in the conversions to racing configurations. The models all had the weight-saving radio delete option, a V10 Tach, dual exhausts with tailpipe extensions, custom lug nuts and center caps, and more goodies.

These cars were awesome on the drag strip with a best run at 10.41 seconds at 141 mph.

One of the ZL-1s was owned by Gibb himself and was campaigned during the 1960s. In the 1970s, Gibb hired Pro Stock driver Jim Hayter who requested that the car be lightened up. An interesting change was the installation of a Rally Sport grille so that the heavy headlight assemblies could be legally removed.

It was a killer setting a record of 9.63 seconds at 143 miles per hour at the AHRA World Points Finals in Fremont, California in 1971.

Yenko Turbo Vega

By 1970, it was evident that the Big-Three automakers were no longer going to build high-performance cars. Due to the rising cost of gasoline, new federal fuel emissions laws and the ever spiraling insurance costs, the days of factory high performance cars just weren't going to happen anymore.

Don Yenko hated the prospect and decided that he would build some Chevy high performance cars on his own again, adding to the reputation he had made

Chevy's Stable					
Weight figures for Chevrolet lightweights					
	1963	1964	1965	1966	1967
Impala SS	3,390 lbs.	3,450 lbs.	3,570 lbs.	3,485 lbs.	3,615 lbs.
Chevelle Malibu SS	–	2,975 lbs.	3,115 lbs.	3,375 lbs.	3,415 lbs.
Chevy II / Nova SS	2,590 lbs.*	2,675 lbs.	2,690 lbs.	2,740 lbs.	2,690 lbs.
Corvair Monza	2,415 lbs.*	2,470 lbs.*	2,440 lbs.*	2,445 lbs.*	2,465 lbs.*

*These cars were produced with six-cylinder engines. Drag racers inserted V-8 engines.
In 1967, the Camaro V-8 coupe was introduced with a weight of 2,890 lbs.
Source: *Standard Catalog of Chevrolet.*

with Yenko Camaros and Novas earlier. To that end, he looked at the tiny 1971 Vega, a small four-cylinder economy car. The performance-oriented dealer looked at the vehicle and visualized what it could be with big-time power.

As if it wasn't already light enough, Yenko indicated that he would lighten it up either further with the substitution of fiberglass front and rear spoilers. And in order to kick up the horses, the Vega would now be carrying a turbocharger that kicked up the output to an impressive 155 horses. The set-up only weighed about 2,700 pounds.

Don was thinking what the souped-up Vega would be able to do on the drag strip, but then the EPA found out what Don had in mind. The agency informed Don that the now-named "Yenko Turbo Vega" would have to pass EPA certification before it could be sold to the public.

To receive the certification, it would be necessary for the car to run a 50,000-mile test run, something that Yenko was ready to do initially, before deciding at the last minute not to go through with it. Yenko went ahead and produced the model as the Yenko Vega, but it didn't come with the turbocharger. That had to be purchased separately.

Few of these cars were built, and even fewer remain today.

Pro Stock Vegas

Although the Vega came a few years after the 1960s Super Stock/ lightweight era, the fascination with the light body that was capable of carrying a V-8 power plant found its way into Pro Stock racing during the 1970s.

Again, Bill "Grumpy" Jenkins was the man with a small-block-Chevy under the hood of his Vega. In the 1972 Winternationals, for example, Jenkins cut a hole shot and flipped off a 9.68-second/140.18-mph run.

Chapter 3

DODGE
LIGHTWEIGHTS

The world of Dodge lightweight racing was one of high publicity and great success. Although the effort was closely aligned with the Plymouth, Dodge maintained an identity of its own. When most recall that golden era, the Dodge name brings up the legendary "Ramcharger" drag team and of course, the powerful Hemi power plant.

Background

Through the 1950s, Chrysler certainly was not behind in the development of powerful engines. The development of the Hemi engine was underway in the 331-, 354-, and 392-cubic inch sizes that gave an idea of what was to come in the 1960s. When that decade did come, there was the famous family of Wedge engines that helped Dodge monopolize on the strips early.

1961-The Beginnings

This restored 1963 "Candymatic" Dodge recalls a time over four decades ago when these cars were supreme.

It really started quite innocently. A group of young Dodge engineers, led by Dick Maxwell, put together a drag team they thought could compete on the national level.

"The thing that really pushed corporate involvement was the emphasis that was being put on [drag racing] by the competition—primarily Pontiac," recalled Maxwell.

A constant Dodge performance advocate was Mr. Norm's Grand-Spaulding dealership that sponsored this Charger.

Bob Plumer

That would certainly prove to be an understatement as the team contended for the next decade.

The early success of the Ramchargers team encouraged Chrysler's drag racing exposure throughout the decade. In addition to the Ramchargers team, Chrysler Corporation had further involvement in drag racing, according to Maxwell.

"We had somewhere between 44 and 50 cars under parts contracts around the country...in the mid 1960s," Maxwell said.

The first Ramcharger effort was in 1961 when they selected a 1961 Dodge with a 413-cid, 375-hp Wedge engine under the hood. There was apparently no vehicle lightening accomplished, but that would certainly change in the immediate years to come.

1962 Dodge Lightweights

Although there was no aftermarket lightening done on the '62 models, they came out lighter anyway, coming mostly from the fact that they were of unibody construction, so there was no heavy frame.

That, plus the fact that the models were smaller, effectively lopped off considerable weight. What happened was that Chrysler downsized its 1962 models and that effectively lopped off 300 to 500 pounds. It was like getting a ton of performance for nothing. Add the new Max Wedge Ramcharger engine (the same engine that Plymouth named the 413 Super Stock), with its 410 and 420 horsepower ratings, and you had a super-potent combination.

The production models also included an extensive use of aluminum, including the dash and even the starter motor. In the race versions, the teams used lightweight tube engine headers.

The tranny of choice for competition was the 727 TorqueFlite automatic.

Not surprisingly, the results were definitely on the positive side with many wins in NHRA Super Stock racing. Similar success was being enjoyed with their

An historic photo showing dualing Ramchargers Dodges.

Bob Plumer

counterpart Plymouths, but it was like they were different companies as each had their own following.

"We were dominant with the Wedge cars, once we got them worked out," said Maxwell. "We were better because we were all engineers and analyzed what was happening to the cars. We had the edge in that we had the training to understand why [things would happen] and could take it to the next step."

There was a significant sign of things to come, both from the driver and a national win. The driver was Elton "Al" Eckstrand, who would be a huge player in the soon-to-follow Ramchargers team.

A Chrysler Corporation lawyer, he had raced Chrysler 300s in the late 1950s and would drive his own "Res Ipsa Loquitor" Dodge in match drag races as well.

"To me, drag racing was like the knights of legend," he recalled. "You came with valor and chivalry to a joust or sword fight and at the end of that short encounter one of the two challengers would be victorious."

Later, Eckstrand would become well known as a driver in the Plymouth Golden Commandos race team and for his Plymouth dragster, "Lawman."

The impressive win for the Ramchargers was the Super Stock Automatic Class at the 1962 NHRA Nationals. The Ramchargers earned a reputation for winning.

AL ECKSTRAND
TOP STOCK ELIMINATOR
1963 NHRA WINTERNATIONALS

BOLD CONFIDENCE as he puts experimental Hurst floor shift for automatics through the gears.

Al smiles proudly and rightfully so after he skillfully and dramatically drove his 1963 Dodge through the tremendous competition to become top Stock Eliminator at Pomona February 17th, 1963.

"'Jump Away", "Go Away", "Magic Go", "The Fastest, the Bestest" — the fancy names and claims for shifters ramble on and on, but when it comes to all out performance and the stakes are high, I put my shifting problems in the hands of only one, Mr. Hurst."

Take it from the champions and the nation's leading automobile makers. Don't gamble with that valuable transmission, or your driving pleasure. Put your faith in Mr. Hurst. Under his supervision transmission controls of all types are under constant development and only after rigid testing and careful evaluation does i.. release them for production and sale.

Al Eckstrand

JUNE 1963

HURST
Hurst-Campbell, Inc.
Glenside, Pa.

21

This June 1963 Hot Rod ad shows Ramchargers driver Al Eckstrand, a Chrysler Corporation lawyer by day, in a Hurst shifter ad.

"There were massive egos in that group," Tom Hoover recalled in a 1997 article written at their reunion by Tom Condran. "They worked together to achieve the known objective. It's a matter of ego satisfaction because the group succeeds."

1963 Dodge Lightweights

This year, Dodge got serious about making their models lighter. Aluminum was selected as the material of choice. The metal was substituted for steel on the lower front body, splash pan, hood (including the hood scoop) and front fenders. Radio and heater delete, deletion of sound deadener, a lightweight steel bumper, and no body undercoating also shaved off some pounds.

A *Hot Rod* photo essay in May 1963 included a photo of the aluminum front-end parts laid out in pieces like the parts from a model kit including fenders, hood and all bumper parts. The essay showed how holes in the hood matched the Dodge engine. Finally, an assembled lightweight front with aluminum bumpers was shown with the claim that 150 pounds was trimmed.

The expected movement of the battery to the trunk also took place along with deleting all the factory carpeting and padding. A skinny rubber mat was the replacement. Finally, the lightest Dodge two-door sedan available, the Dodge 330, at 3,238 pounds, was selected to take off 50 more pounds. The lightweight installation actually transferred about two percent of the car's weight to the rear of the car.

The Ramcharger engine was now 426 cubic inches, derived from boring out the 413 Wedge power plant.

A 1963 Dodge lightweight. These unit-bodied, factory-produced cars were top drag racers.

DODGE'S RAMCHARGERS
Some Thoughts...

Some days you win

Some days you lose

The fortunes on the straight and narrow warpath change as quickly as the gears in the go-box! Today you tear 'em up. Tomorrow is another day. Your machine has got to be mean . . . you've got to be good . . . and you've got to come out of the hole with more togetherness than Amos and Andy! That's the drama of the drag strip, man and machine.

That's why more than 200,000 buffs bulged the track at Indy for the NHRA's big showdown—the world championships. And what a showdown! On Saturday, Jim Thornton in a '63 Dodge downed his Ramcharger teammate, Herman Mozer, on his

way to royalty in the Super Stock Automatic Class. Next day, running for the meet's most coveted honor—Top Stock Eliminator—Mozer turned the tables and gave Thornton the thumb. But the event was far from over. Mozer still had to face the present "Mr. Eliminator," Al Eckstrand in Lawman, another specially equipped '63 Dodge. And another winner is defeated. Mozer edged him by 1-100th of a second with an e.t. of 12.22.

Some days you win. Some days you lose. That's what keeps the quarter-mile jaunt so interesting. But have you noticed? When a Dodge loses these days . . . it's to another Dodge.

Hot Dodge

DODGE DIVISION ✦ CHRYSLER MOTORS CORPORATION

They worked on Chrysler Corporation projects by day, then got together for drag racing pursuits in their free time. They drove Dodges in competition and became known as the Ramchargers. Along the way, they became drag racing legends.

Both Tom Hoover began at Chrysler Corporation in 1955 and was an original member of the Ramchargers while Bob Cahill joined in later. Their thoughts are excerpted from the *Dodge Forum* (Hoover) and *Mopar Performance News*, October 1995 (Cahill).

"In the very beginning, it was me and Wayne Erickson...and probably Herb Moser and Dan Mancini were the others. We formed the club in 1958," Hoover recalled.

"I won my class at the national drags in 1960 with an early Hemi."

Chrysler Corporation encouraged the Ramchargers and realized success would promote Dodge and Plymouth to a growing generation of potential buyers.

"We set out to make a national drag racing performance package," said Hoover, noting that Chrysler chairman Lynn Townsend was behind the effort. By the spring of 1962, both Plymouth and Dodge introduced cars that carried a wallop.

"They were successful right off the bat," claimed Hoover. "They would run 110 in the quarter or something close to that right off the showroom floor!"

The Ramchargers drag racing team was ready to race competition versions of the spirited cars.

"...we put extra time into not only coming up with better equipment, but spreading the word that Chrysler products were the coming thing in the Super Stock wars," said Cahill.

"The first community effort was the 'High and Mighty' car," said Hoover. "Dodge asked how much we would want. It became the Ramchargers Dodge at that point. [It was] a band of brothers—8 or 10 people [who] were very serious about it."

"By working with various departments in the plant, they very quickly picked up on the latest ideas and applied them to their own racing," said Cahill.

"As soon as they were track proven," he added, "they were given a factory part number and made available at a very nominal expense to all the racers."

"When we got to '63, and put the aluminum nose on, those cars just dominated stock car drag racing," said Hoover.

Chrysler progress also came from NASCAR racing and the progression from the Max Wedge to the 1960s Hemi V-8. Success led to the Hemi being introduced to drag racing and to the public.

"I ran my street Hemi on occasion," recalled Hoover. "It would run 117 track speed at the drags on the street tires."

One other offshoot of the Ramcharger racing was education.

"For the 15 years, I conducted what we called the Racers Seminar Series every spring," said Hoover. "We would try to hit the population centers...stay the weekend and visit a few of the aftermarket suppliers..."

The Ramchargers left a proud, visible legacy for Dodge, Plymouth and the overall Chrysler Corporation.

"It was kind of the Ramcharger type of thing," noted Hoover. "We did hobby type activities that would complement what we were trying to do for the Chrysler. I was always very proud of what we were able to accomplish."

This vintage color image shows a Ramcharger's light weight in action.
Bob Plumer

1963 Ramcharger
Specifications

Headers:	A lightweight pair specially tuned, attached to 48-inch lengths of tubular steel pipes.
Ignition:	A factory-installed Mopar ignition system.
Plugs:	Champion J9Y or for problem cylinders, Champion J10Y
Carburetion:	Carter AFB dual carbs (Carter No. 3447 SA)
Fuel pump:	Two Bendix electric supplementary pumps (Bendix No. 476459)
Air cleaner:	Air filter bottoms used to shape and direct air flow to the carburetor.
Water pump/ fan:	The seven-blade air conditioning fan plus viscous drive unit was used although they endorsed the standard 18-inch, four-blade fan and water pump.
Heads:	Heads were in the 81 to 84 cc range.
Camshaft:	A properly timed camshaft with an accurate lash setting.
Deck height:	A surface finish of the block deck and cylinder head in a 100 to 120 micro-inch range.
Pan:	Lowered to increase oil capacity to six quarts (from five).
Transmission:	Checked to verify adjustments of kickdown, low and reverse bands, line pressure and the throttle linkage to the transmission.
Tires:	*FRONT*: Goodyear Sports Car Special 6.75 x 15 six-ply tires
	REAR: M & H Super Stock 9.00 x 14 or 15 tires, depending on track conditions
Differential:	4.30, 4.56 and 4.89 ratios
Chassis:	Proper wheel balance and alignment to prevent any vibration.
Lubricants:	SAE 30 weight oil used for speed trials. Maintain all grease and oiled fittings.
Front end:	Dodge-made aluminum fenders, hood with air scoop, front bumper and supports, carburetor air intake ducts, and stone and splash shields.
Battery:	A 90-amp, 60-pound battery (25 lbs. more than stock) is mounted in the trunk.

In addition, there were also improvements made to the cylinder heads and new 13.5-1 high-dome pistons.

Actually, the just-described 1963 Dodge Lightweight was the work of 15 Chrysler engineers and technicians. The work was done after hours to ready their new 426 Ramcharger power plant for the 1963 Winternationals. That Dodge team would double as the Ramchargers team.

This equipment almost didn't make it for the 1963 season. It was stamped out just before the company shut down to prepare for 1964 production. Eckstrand quickly showed the car was ready as he took the Winternationals Top Stock Class with a 12.44 clocking. The excellence continued with Ramcharger team member Herman Mozer taking the 1963 Nationals in an even-better 12.22 second E.T.

The Ramcharger cars were hard to miss with the team name stretched along each side in large slanted red letters. But the real trademark of the team was the peppermint stripe motif of the top of the car. The view of those rear deck stripes were a familiar view to competitors as Ramcharger Dodges pulled away to another victory.

Guess it goes without saying that these cars were NOT intended for street use. There even was an underhood tag that warned, "Caution-This car is equipped with a maximum performance engine."

In a June 1963 *Hot Rod* profile, the Ramchargers featured, including Dan Mancini, Jim Thornton, Mike Buckel, Tom Hoover, Al Eckstrand, Kaye Larkin, Steve Baker, Tom Coddington and Gary Congdon offered this "recipe" for a Ramcharger lightweight.

"The car was tuned better than a Swiss watch," noted the *Hot Rod* article. "The car is tuned to deliver maximum performance. The driver tunes himself to the car."

Before the 1960s Hemi, the choice of Dodge racers was the Max Wedge V-8.

In the same issue, Ramchargers team member and drive Al Eckstrand offered tips on driving a high performance car such as focusing on the flag holder, gripping the shifter, following one's senses, and not watching the other driver.

"I have always felt that I'd rather be lucky than be fast," said Eckstrand. "Make my car attractive and safe so lady luck will want to ride with me."

The 1964 Mancini Racing Dodge SS featured unique "peppermint stripe" paint.
Mancini Photos

1964 Dodge Lightweights

The transition year for the Dodge Lightweight cars was 1964. That transition mainly involved the engine compartment where there was a power plant changing during the season.

The season started with the 426 Ramcharger (the Max Wedge), but in February of 1964, Chrysler introduced the 426 Hemi V-8. Its heritage was the 1950s Chrysler Red Ram Hemi engine. The basic 426 Ramcharger block was used with the Hemi, but with cross-bolt mains and heavier webbing added. But when the unique Hemi heads were added, it came together with over 500 horses being produced. A tuned Hemi, with an aluminum induction set-up mounting two four-barrel carbs, was capable of 700 horsepower.

"We were given the task of coming up with a conversion of the big block [Wedge] V-8 engine," recalled

chief engineer Bill Weertman, who explained that draftsman Frank Bilk drew the conversion. "It applied the same type of head and valves we had used on the hemispherical engine of the 1950s. It was a truly rush program that took all of our energies to get the parts for a build of the first engine in November."

"It was a great sound when that engine fired up with a great big va-ROOM," Weertman added.

The lightweight aspects of the car were continued this year with a custom-fabricated aluminum hood with a single inlet scoop, lightweight front bumper/fenders and doors, support/ lower valance and magnesium front wheels, a lightweight Dodge van seat, Lexan side windows. Also, there was only one windshield wiper and no sun visors or sound deadening.

So why didn't they have an aluminum rear bumper? Simple, they wanted as much weight as possible over the rear wheels. For the same reason, standard sheet metal was used from the doors on back.

An interesting change was made to the model when the much heavier Hemi replaced the Wedge engine, a program that received the factory designation of A990. Aluminum doors and hinges were reportedly offered to counter the additional Hemi weight.

During this period, there was also a factory effort to lighten the Hemi as much as possible. Areas addressed included using aluminum in a number of areas, such as the cylinder heads, oil pump body, water pump housing, and other locations. Magnesium was used to fabricate the intake manifold. It was common knowledge at the time that the Hemi was putting out 75 to 125 more horsepower than the 427 Fords.

Like other lightweights of the era, there was also a warning about keeping the 1964 Dodge lightweight off

The "king" in Dodge engine bays before the 426 Hemi was this awesome 426 Wedge engine.

Another angle shows the Dodge Wedge engine with the dual air cleaner covers removed.

Another famous 1960s Dodge was the Hemi-powered "Honker."

Bob Plumer

the public streets. In this application, the warning read, "Designed for use in supervised acceleration trials. It is not recommended for general every day driving because of the compromise of all-around characteristics which must be made for this type of vehicle."

Among those cars, there were the unforgettable Dick Landy driven "Automotive Research" Super Stockers. An early version was the Stage III Ramcharger-powered Dodge Polara Super Stock also driven by Landy. The Polara was a popular choice because of the sleeker body style.

Because of his obvious prestige and position, Landy was one of the first to acquire one of the Hemi-powered models. The monster power plant sat in the engine compartment of a Dodge 330.

But Landy was never satisfied with cars when he received them. He constantly looked for more weight reductions, and it wasn't surprising to have frame members drilled out and body panels acid-dipped.

(And it's not surprising that just two years later, in 1966, Landy would race in a 1,700-pound Dodge Dart two-door complete with acetate windows, aluminum engine mounts, tube framing, .60-inch aluminum flooring, plus fiberglass fenders, hood and deck.)

Landy was like many other super stars of the 1960s Super Stock days by jumping around amongst brands when one looked like it had a performance edge. Early in his career, Landy raced a 1962 406-cid powered lightweight Galaxie, before spending two years in Wedge-powered Plymouths. He ran the Dodge nametag

Dodge promoted its Ramchargers team in this 1964 factory drag racing flyer. *Phil Hall Collection*

in 1964, a year when Chrysler products dominated the Super Stock class.

The "Color Me Gone" was an early 1964 Dodge Super Stocker 426 Wedge car, driven by Roger Lindamood, that is well remembered because of that catchy name. It won the NHRA Nationals in the Top Stock Class that year.

"Color Me Gone" has been restored in replica form but using some of the original parts. During its competition days, it was modified and cobbled up a bunch. In fact, for the 1965 season, it was turned into an altered wheelbase model.

The "Hemi Honker" was another notable 1964 Dodge lightweight that competed in the NHRA Super Stock Automatic class with Bud Faubel at the wheel. The car was a regular winner and held an NHRA record at one time. A consistent low-11 performer, its best effort was an 11.20 second dash at 125+ miles per hour.

Another feather in Dodge's cap during the 1964 season was the winning of the Super Stock Automatic Class at the Nationals by a Ramchargers Dodge 330 SS car with Jim Thornton at the wheel.

But there was one other drag accomplishment for Dodge during that long-ago summer. The effort

one for the strip... and one for the street

426 CU. IN. ramcharger V-8

426 CU. IN. high performance V-8

One of the hottest power plants ever to come off a production line. Specially engineered features, combined with top engine displacement, put the Ramcharger in a class by itself. Firmly established as a leading contender for top honors on sanctioned drag strips across the nation. In '64 it's the one to beat!

This big new Dodge V-8 "street" engine has been developed from the highly successful 426 Ramcharger which currently dominates the nation's drag strips. It has the extra punch that the high-performance fan wants, yet it is suitable for around town driving.

Dodge promotional materials touted two hefty 426-cid racing engines. *Phil Hall Collection*

involved the use of a period Hemi power plant equipped with a GMC 6-71 supercharger that enabled the production of up to 900 horsepower at 7,800 rpm on a lightweight Dodge.

Weight was always a concern in the engine compartment, thus lightweight Weiand magnesium intake manifolds were employed on the powerful Dodge.

Keeping the chassis weight down was also a design goal and it was aided by actually removing both bumpers (giving it a very sleek appearance). The use of lightweight American Racing alloy wheels and removal of sheet metal (aluminum was freely substituted on the Dodge's body) provided a greater radius on each wheel well. The outboard headlights were removed and served as giant air ducts, giving the front end an almost sinister look.

Three of the Dodges constructed were called the Chargers, prior to the time when that name would have an entirely different meaning for Dodge lovers with the introduction of the stunning new 1966 Charger. The drag racing Chargers were prepared for Dodge by Dragmaster Corporation of Carlsbad, California, these special Dodge Chargers were sponsored in regional exhibitions by various Dodge dealer associations.

The Dodges were painted red, white and blue, with darker sides and the white showing up on the hood, top and trunk lid. They featured a custom tail pan treatment that made them attractive and unusual looking cars front and back.

The effort received a lot of publicity in national advertisements that showed the Dodge with a huge parachute deployed and trailing out behind it. It also set a new speed record of 135.33 miles per hour in the quarter at Tucson Dragway in Arizona.

1965 Dodge Lightweights (Super Stock)

With the success that Dodge had enjoyed the previous years, the 1965 season could best be described as a continuation of that momentum. In the engine department, the evolution continued with the substitution of magnesium intakes replacing aluminum, along with aluminum also being the standard cylinder head material.

The Dodge "Color Me Gone" was driven by Roger Lindamood.

This 1964 Dodge was used in competition by Dick Landy. Mike Mueller

The Coronet was the body style of choice for the 1965 Super Stock Dodges. It was identified with the WO1 designation. A surprising change in the front end was that aluminum became a lightweight material of the past. The change was to thinner steel sheet metal, the doors for example were only .018 inch thick, as were the hood, hood scoop, and fenders. The change came as a result of an NHRA rule change. However, aluminum was used in the oil pump housing, heads, and door hinges.

And there certainly wasn't much front-end protection as the bumpers were only .040 inches thick with the thickness of the Corning safety glass measuring only 1/8 inch.

There was still continuing effort to lighten the interior with the back seat being removed along with the door arm rests. There were also no sun visors, sound deadener, along with the normal radio- and heater-delete. In an interesting change, the shifter moved from the floor to the steering column replacing the push-button style of 1964. The frames that supported the single Dodge van seat were aluminum with sizable holes drilled in them for additional lightness.

These cars got trimmed down even further with such minimal items as the dash liner, cowl side trim panels, coat hooks and dome light all not being installed. Underneath, there were no front sway bars, and the torsion bars from a six-cylinder engine set-up. Finally, the wheelbase was shortened by one inch.

The performance was again outstanding as the AHRA Top Stock Eliminator Class was taken by one of the 1965 Ramcharger Dodges, this one piloted by Mike Buckel. Bud Faubel was also on top of the Mr.

Stock Eliminator class, while Bob Harrop took the Super Stock Automatic at the NHRA Nationals.

The production for 1965 was sizable with 200 Dodge Super Stockers, or 40 more than the Plymouth version.

1965 Dodge Lightweights (Factory Experimental Class)

In addition to the Super Stock versions, there were also a half dozen Dodge altered wheelbase cars built during this model year. NHRA had a factory expert when these cars appeared for competition. They were found far too radical to compete in that class and were disallowed.

But, they went ahead and raced with the AHRA association with fans loving them. The cars would also do a lot of match racing drawing huge crowds.

"We were faced with a situation of having to race against the new Ford cammer in 106-inch wheelbase Mustangs, which had a much better traction than our stock wheelbase of 115 inches," Bob Cahill of Chrysler recalled in 1995.

Ramcharger driver Jim Thornton had come up with a concept of a two-percent forward adjustment in 1964 and looked at the concept again in 1965. Now the plan was to move the front and rear wheels forward 10 to 15 inches.

"I just thought if a little bit was good, a bunch more would be even better," said Thornton.

Twelve cars were built, including one "mule" version that wasn't raced.

While these new "funny cars" (because their altered wheelbase made them funny looking) were banned from competition, they soon ran exhibitions or match races that got everyone's attention. While Fords had won the Winternationals with a 10.8-second run, Dick Landy ran his new Dodge in 10.26 seconds in an exhibition that March in Bakersfield, California.

Those who got the new Dodge funny cars were Landy, Bobby Harrop ("The Flying Carpet"), Bud Faubel ("Hemi Honker"), Dave Strickler, Jim Thornton and Mike Buckel ("Ramchargers"), and Roger Lindamood ("Color Me Gone"). There would also be a number of the A/FX cars built by different teams, along with some conversions of Super Stock models.

The factory Dodge A/FX cars were actually achieved by modifying existing Super Stockers, and the word "modifying" should be emphasized because the resulting A/FX cars were a far, far cry from the starting point.

The cars were stripped down and were acid-dipped which reduced the weight by some 200 pounds. Unlike the Super Stock cars, the A/FX models were too complicated to be built on a production line. No doubt about it, these were out-and-out race cars.

The custom lower frame rails and relocation of the wheel wells allowed the front wheels to assume their new forward location. Along with this maneuver, the shock mount and upper control arm pivot were moved 10 inches forward.

Guess it goes without saying that the relocation required major modifications to the steering system and torsion bars.

Out back, there was a huge amount of sheet metal and power train modifications to also move the rear wheels forward.

As if the car wasn't already light enough, much of the existing sheet metal was discarded and replaced with fiberglass pieces, namely the doors, rear deck lid, hood, and even the front bumper and dashboard.

Needless to say, the A/FX Dodges were considerably lighter than the SS cars, coming in at an amazing 2,800 pounds. With that minimal weight figure, it's certainly not surprising to learn there were quarter-mile speeds in the 140-mph range.

Both the 1965 Super Stock and A/FX Dodges continued to use the powerful Hemi A990 engine. It continued to be refined and improved, and reportedly was cranking out well over 500 horses in factory race trim.

An area of major upgrading occurred in the induction system with the 1965 introduction of a Hilborn fuel injection system. Several different velocity stack heights were used. With the new fuel injection system, Landy became the first person to hit 150 mph in an unblown stock drag racer.

Dick Landy's 1965 Dodge, ready to run. Mike Mueller

The "Landy's Dodge" A/FX machine was possibly the most significant of the few factory machines. One reason for its success was that Landy was able to reduce the overall weight by an additional 300 pounds under the factory weight figure.

Originally equipped with a four-speed, Landy changed it to a TorqueFlite automatic transmission and equipped the power plant with fuel injection. His accomplishments included the winning of the Cecil County Drag-O-Way All Star event, turning a new record of 9.59-second/143+ mph. Then came the 1965 Super Stock Nationals where there was a winning 9.52/143.54 effort. That marvelous season was Landy's only one with the funny car Dodge. He sold the car to one of his former mechanics.

The car is now in the possession of AWB expert Mike Guffey who spent great time and effort to restore it back to its 1965 configuration.

Others had success with their Dodges as well. In August 1965, Jim Thornton ran a remarkable time of 9.19, then topped it with an 8.91-second run. Independent Gary Dyer, in a Dodge altered supercharged and prepared by Mr. Norm's Grand-Spaulding Dodge, ran an 8.63-second time that summer at Lion's Drag Strip.

1966 Lightweight Dodges

This season saw the return of the AWB cars to NHRA. The new class was called XS, for Experimental Stock that brought out the old A/FX

The 1966 Hoover Hemi-powered Dodge was a special car. This one has a unique floor shifter (above left). The famed Hemi V-8 filled the engine bay (above right). Tom Glatch

The "Rambunctious" lightweight AWB car began life as a wrecked 1965 Dodge Dart.

cars from the previous year.

As far as competition in NHRA events, most of the Chrysler Corporation success was accomplished by Plymouths. The only success in the 1966 Nationals was a 1965 Dodge Dart driven by Gene Snow in the Competition Eliminator Class.

Corporately, Chrysler pulled back a bit from the advances the altered Dodges had made in 1965, with a sales perspective in mind.

"We were forced to run injectors and nitro methane because everyone else was doing it and everything was happening so fast," recalled Maxwell in 1995. "...our business was to race what we sold and the funny cars were very far removed from what we offered in our dealers' showrooms."

Landy's potent '66 Dart Lightweight was one of only two factory sponsored funny cars that year. He constructed the lightweight machine with a square tube frame and a significant engine setback. He competed with the Dart for about four months and indicated that it was very successful. In May 1996, a *Hot Rod* photo feature on the Landy Dart reported times of just a bit over 8.9 seconds.

One other 1966 Lightweight deserves attention for its accomplishments and advanced technology. It was constructed by Gene Snow strictly for match racing. The "Rambunctious" altered wheelbase car began life as a wrecked '65 Dodge Dart and did considerable match racing that year. There was no significant lightening done on the car for that season, but that situation would quickly change.

The Ramchargers again campaigned a funny car version of the Dart but their car was prepared by Woody Gilmore. Like the Landy car, their Dart ran in the low 8-second range, reportedly.

For the 1966 season, the modifications were significant and produced basically a factory-style A/

FX machine. The front end was lengthened and the body was fitted with fiberglass components with all the window glass removed. When it was completed, the unique Dart weighed a very-minimal 2,300 pounds.

The interior was completely gutted with the only significant item being a bucket seat. Power came from a Hilborn injected stock displacement Hemi exhausted by super-long Zoomie Headers.

The 727 TorqueFlite automatic was shifted by the old reliable push-buttons. Even though the car was mostly match-raced in the southwest, it was able to win the NHRA Nationals in the 1966 Competition Eliminator and 1967 Super Eliminator Classes.

1967 Lightweight Dodges

Although the year was 1967, the old '65 Super Stock Dodges were still showing their stuff. In the A Stock Automatic class at the 1967 Nationals, a two-year-old model was driven to victory by Leonard Hughes.

But Chrysler also had what was referred to as the WO23, which was a number (55 to be exact) of a lightweight Dodge Coronet 440 two-door hardtop. Plymouth would have a similar program (the RO23) that was an identically-equipped Belvedere II model.

The cars were designed to run in the B Stock class, but NHRA would have the final say and mandated that the class be with D Stock. The big teams would only use these cars for a single year before the ultimate lightweight Dodge machine would appear the following year.

With the expected 426 Hemi in place, the remainder of the power train was a four-speed manual transmission and a Dana 60 rear end.

But it was the rest of the package that really set the WO23 apart. The interior was completely cleaned

THE DODGE BOYS:
Dandy and the Snowman

Over the years, two drivers led the way for Dodge racing success. Californian Dick Landy and Texan Gene Snow kept Dodge in drag racing headlines.

Landy began drag racing a Ford pickup in the 1950s and drove Fords until he switched to a 1962 Plymouth Max Wedge. His career took off in 1964 when he drove a lightweight Dodge hardtop. In 1965, he was one of the first to have an altered Dodge Hemi production car.

"I worked the car down to 2,500 lbs.," he recalled in a 1970 interview with *Hot Rod* writer John Dianna.

An engineering student at the University of Texas at Arlington, Gene Snow left to sell used cars. While some talked about it, Snow *did* race on Sunday and sell cars on Monday.

"I would win a race...and usually sold the winning entry the next day," Snow recalled.

He raced Chevrolets until 1962 when he switched to a Plymouth Sport Fury. He progressed to a Hemi Dodge in 1964. In 1965, he began

Bob Plumer

a streak of wins with his altered wheelbase "Rambunctious" Dodge Dart.

"There's an instant during a funny car ride where it feels just like the first downhill plunge on a roller coaster," Snow told *Hot Rod* in 1971. "...I like the sensation of being scared."

The Dodge Boys piled up successes. Landy won 12 match

races in 1966 while Snow broke the 200 and 210 mph barriers in 1968 with his Dart. Along the way, Landy led many Dodge-sponsored clinics.

"It was certainly the most professional program that I had ever been associated with," Landy told *Mopar Performance* in 1995. "I think it was one of Chrysler's most significant steps taken in their racing operations."

Bob Plumer

Landy, famous for his ever-present cigar, said he never smoked.

"I just chew on 'em and throw 'em away," he told *Hot Rod* in 1971. "I chew a box a week when I'm racing."

Landy, who raced until 1980, runs Dick Landy Industries in Northridge, California, and continues to promote Mopar Performance engines and performance parts.

Snow finished in the NHRA Top 10 nine times between 1983 and 1991. He now runs an A/Fuel Dragster on a hobby basis.

Neither blew smoke—or snowflakes—on the strip. Their Dodges just left drivers in the dust.

Top Left: *M and H Racemaster Tires featured the Ramchargers Dodge in their ad.* Phil Hall Collection

Top Middle: *Gene "the Snowman" Snow was one of a series of famous drag racers on Fram posters.* Phil Hall Collection

Top Right: *Dick Landy and his trademark cigar (for chewing, not smoking) in a Cragar wheel ad.*

Bob Plumer

out to the bare essentials. There were no wheel covers, body sealing material, body insulation, radio or heater.

Although the cars were austerely equipped, the Coronets still had pretty much of a factory look about them with all the standard body chrome in place. For some unknown reason, these models faired poorly against the company competition in Plymouth who garnered a number of national titles.

That might have been the case for the Stock classes, but there was one match-race gasser called the "Mr. Norm's Super Charger" of the famous Grand-Spaulding Dodge operation. The model carried a stock-appearing 1967 Dodge Charger fiberglass body which weighed in at only 220 pounds, along with a 250-pound chrome-moly AWB frame. Both the battery and fuel tank were located past the rear axle for more weight on the rear wheels. The driveline consisted of a 727 TorqueFlite automatic equipped with a Dodge A-100 tail shaft.

Power came from the expected Hemi engine equipped with a supercharger that was 25 percent overdriven. That engine, by the way, was moved far rearward for traction improvement.

The NHRA expanded Super Stock Eliminator to 10 classes in 1967 opening the door to more possibilities for cars like the Dodge R/T 440 and Hemi V-8s. Any cams, including those with rollers, were allowed as were larger wheels and tires as long as they fit into fender wells.

1968 Dodge Lightweights

The electricity that would hit the 1968 drag strips was initiated by a late-1967 Dodge Press Release.

"Dodge is putting more zip in its Dart in hopes of hitting the bull's eye in Class B Super Stock drag racing competition this year (1968). The new vehicle, a lighter and quicker '68 Dart hardtop, is featuring the Hemi 426 engine, with production to begin in March."

Not surprisingly, Hurst Performance would be a major player in the builder of this model (and its companion Plymouth Barracuda (which would be equipped identically). As previous experience had proved that lightening was an excellent way to win races, that technique was employed to the hilt in this Dart.

Fiberglass was again the choice for the lightening with the material used in the hood and front fenders. The extensively radiused rear wheel wells again saved weight and accommodated the large rear slicks. Skinny steel was used in the paper-thin doors and even the bumper was considerably thinner than the street version.

There were high-arched rear multi-leaf springs that also helped provide clearance for the growing-

Gene Snow in and Amalie racing oil ad.

This WO23 1967 Dodge Super Stock used the Coronet body style and was one of only 55 built.
Earl Brown

in-size rear slicks, along with the addition of a larger brake system. Up front, there were 11-inch disc brakes, while there were large drums on the front.

The interesting technique of removing the window glass winding mechanism dropped a number of pounds in some cars. A seat belt was strapped to the lower frame of the door to lift and lower the window. All the interior lightening techniques of the past Dodge Super Stock cars were employed, and then some! Of interest, again as in the past, was that the mounts for the lightweight Dodge van seat had been swiss-cheesed with large holes.

Mounting the giant Hemi power plant into the tiny Dart engine compartment was a job of major proportions. It had been necessary to move the master cylinder to the left. For valve cover installation, it was also necessary to redo the shock tower on the right side and modify and slightly relocate the K member.

The standard Hemi power plant was still in position, but it had been refined. A new aluminum cross-ram intake was in place, in addition to a transistor ignition and Hooker Headers. But the most identifiable characteristic of the car was the giant hood scoop that monopolized a large percentage of the hood area.

Both four-speed and TorqueFlite three-speed automatic trannys were available with both being aftermarket units. The manual unit was equipped with the Hurst Competition Shifter. B&M Automotive provided the automatics which carried manual valve bodies and stall converters. For stopping power, the larger brake units from the Coronet model were used.

The first batch of Hemi Darts numbered 50, but it quickly became apparent that the demand was much greater. Thirty of the number were four-speeds. Later, there would be an additional 25 built. But there were certainly many more of the models around, although the other cars weren't produced under company control.

The production process had the partially-completed model from the Hamtramk, Michigan assembly plant to the Hurst facility in Madison Heights, Michigan. Hurst installed the fiberglass pieces and acid-dipped the doors to lighten them. The interior carpet was removed and replaced with a simple rubber mat and the window was replaced with plastic. Hurst also accomplished the window winding mechanism delete.

The turn-key version weighed in at about a ton and one-half of weight. The Darts had an interesting appearance when the customer picked one up. They were done in primer, black from the firewall forward. The remainder of the model was done in grey primer. It looked like it had just been repaired from a front-end accident with a different color front end installed.

Everybody figured that it would be a rocket, and a prototype Hemi Dart proved that to be the case. Right off the bat, it was capable of 10+ seconds and 130 mph performances. Again, Landy was one of the most successful in his Hemi Dart who had his hardest competition being the Plymouth Mopar brothers.

These cars would continue to compete for a number of years after their introduction. And the amazing aspect of these cars is that even in the 21st century, a number of the three and one-half decade Hemi Darts are still doing their thing on the drag strip. Granted, there have been some modern improvements made to the cars enabling them to run in the eight-second range, but they are still basically the same cars.

Chapter 4

FORD
LIGHTWEIGHTS

Ford started early in the Lightweight game and stayed involved most of the decade. A number of models participated including the Galaxie, Fairlane, Falcon, and Mustang in various classes throughout the years.

Dick Brannan, Gas Ronda, Les Ritchey, Don Nicholson, Bill Lawton, Clester Andrews, Len Richter, Butch Leal for Mickey Thompson, Hubert Platt and Phil Bonner were some of the legendary drivers who wheeled the lightweight FoMoCo machines. The cars participated in the Factory Experimental, Super Stock, and other classes as well as Funny car.

Probably the best known factory lightweight, the Thunderbolt, was a Fairlane derivative that incorporated dramatic weight reduction. Today, those few remaining are performance classics of the highest order and bring asking prices into the six-figure category.

Traditionally performance-minded, Ford had started their program by 1960. One example was the 1960 High Performance Galaxie Special 360 model. The 360 horsepower was derived from the basic 352-cubic inch engine with upgraded camshaft, cylinder heads, carburetor and exhaust system. The engine was capable of pushing the three-speed, 3,700-pound model through the quarter mile in 14 seconds at almost 100 mph. Imagine how it would have performed

Gas Ronda and his Davis Ford altered Mustang.

Bob Plumer

A good example of the 1963 Ford Galaxie lightweight was this Ed Martin Ford version.

Bob Plumer

with a four-speed transmission (not an option at the time) and less weight!

Lightweight Galaxies

It's hard to figure why the bulky Galaxie model was selected for the Ford lightweight application. Galaxies were the sales leader at the time and were the company's choice. The Galaxie "light" program lasted for three model years, from 1962 through 1964.

A significant effort to reduce the heavy Galaxie weight by 400 to 500 pounds was undertaken by the Special Vehicles Department team at Ford in Dearborn, Michigan in the Spring of 1962. Because of the late start, the SVD completed only 11 cars by the end of production in August. Production jumped to over 200 Lightweight Galaxies in 1963 serving notice that the "Total Performance" image was underway. 1964 saw the end of the Lightweight Galaxie program as only 57 cars were released and sold, all rare today.

It was difficult for the general public to get one of these competition cars for street use, although they could be acquired from dealerships known to handle performance cars and parts. The Lightweight cars came with stock 427 power plants. Fine tuning and modifications were left up to the new owner or team.

Bob Plumer

These two Galaxie lightweights were driven by Phil Bonner.

One of the earliest Ford high-performance models was this 1960 Starliner. It sported a 406-cid tri-power V-8, one of the biggest engines in the industry.

The exploits of the Galaxie Lightweights really paid sales dividends with the "Win on Sunday, Sell on Monday" motto. Ford liked to call these cars "The Lively Ones."

Because of their desirability, many clones have been constructed through the years, and some are very difficult to discern from the originals. Keep this in mind if you ever plan to buy one so you can make sure you are getting the real thing.

Even though weight reduction in the Lightweight Galaxies was impressive, their performance still suffered when matched against the opposition driving a lighter Chevy or MOPAR machine of the era. Even after weight reduction, the Galaxies still were about 3,500 pounds and carried at least a 100- to 150-pound disadvantage.

1962 Galaxie Lightweights

The production guidelines for the initial Galaxie Lightweight came as a result of a brand new 1962 Galaxie that Dick Brannan had modified and the Brannan Galaxie whipped everybody, including the 421 Pontiacs and the 413-powered Dodges and Plymouths and was still legal.

Much of the pressure to copy Brannan's car ended at Ford Headquarters in Spring 1962 when Les Ritchey, a Ford Performance guru from California, argued that Ford cars in factory trim were just too heavy to compete at the national level. Plans were made to modify some

existing production 406 Galaxie two-door sedans, transforming them into the first Ford Lightweights.

The Galaxies were modified by Dearborn Steel Tubing (DST) of Dearborn, Michigan. The cars were fitted with thinner window glass, plus fiberglass hoods, front fenders, deck lid and lightweight seats, all of which reportedly saved about 400 pounds. Some early data indicated fiberglass doors would be added but that never happened, even though it would have saved another 30 to 35 pounds.

Other modifications included aluminum inner fender panels, front bumper, front and rear bumper brackets, and a special lightweight frame. The radio, heater, clock, armrests and carpet all were deleted. Since there was no spare tire, the jack was omitted. Super thin lightweight rubber floor mats replaced the carpet. Special light bucket front seats replaced the original bench type and all sound sealing was deleted from the body.

These were the real thing and had they been introduced early in the year they surely would have put Ford among the best.

All 1962s were powered by Ford's 406 Tri-Power 405-hp production V-8. In the trunk was a never-before released two four-barrel manifold with two Holley four-barrel carburetors. Although the manifold improved engine performance, advertised horsepower remained the same.

While Ford thought it had built the ultimate NHRA Super Stocker, the NHRA had a different

Jerry Hammes is pictured here with Dick Brannan and the original 1962 406 Galaxie along with a new super-lightweight Galaxie, #823, in August 1962.

view. Brannan explained, "NHRA declared the cars non-production requiring entry into the new Factory Experimental Class (A/FX and B/FX) where they did not perform very well having been prepared earlier for a different class."

1963 1/2 Galaxie Lightweights

In 1963, the body style moved to the two-door hardtop "Fastback" model. Except for a few early cars, all were white with red interior, the 427-cubic inch production engine, 4-speed manual transmission and lots of aluminum and fiberglass. They had aluminum lightweight front bumpers and brackets, fiberglass front-end pieces and a lighter aluminum four-speed Borg-Warner transmission accompanied with a 34-pound R & C aluminum scatter proof bell housing. Reportedly, the first 25 cars even had deleted dome lights.

In July 1963, *Hot Rod* magazine reported. "A standard production Galaxie Fastback with bucket seat interior, power windows, radio, heater and 427 high performance engine with accompanying heavy-

duty suspension components weighs 4,150 pounds ... The special lightweight model tips the scales at just 3,480 pounds ready to drag."

In their 1963 article, *Hot Rod* observed two 1963 Ford Lightweights in action. The Les Ritchey version, built before fiberglass doors and inner fender wells were used, did a 12.29-second quarter mile with a top speed of 117.3 mph. A lighter version, equipped with additional fiberglass, was driven by Gas Ronda and hit 118.04 mph in a 12.07-second quarter mile.

The prototype of the '63-1/2 lightweight was built using the 1962 Brannan Ford's lightweight chassis—identical to the planned production version—and was allowed a head start so further development could get underway. Brannan, and veteran Ford Engineer Homer Perry, along with

---

Below: *Clear information was contained on this Galaxie lightweight plate inside the glove compartment door. It explained this car did not meet the high-quality Ford appearance standards.*

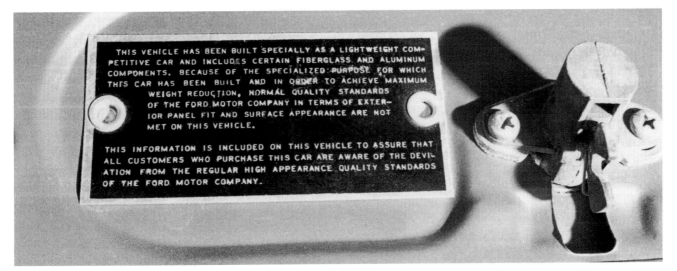

1963-1/2 Ford Lightweight Package	
Frame:	Ford 300 series (lighter gauge steel)
Body:	No sound deadener used.
Fiberglass:	Doors, trunk lid, hood, front fenders, inner fenders
Interior:	Thin, pad-less rubber floor mat (thin as a newspaper). Very simple, lightly padded bucket seats. Radio, heater, clock, etc. not available.
Engine:	Ford 427-cid, 425 hp V-8 with cast aluminum manifold
Transmission:	Aluminum main casing
Miscellaneous:	Heavy-duty springs, shocks and 15-inch wheels
Weight:	3,425 lbs. (with fiberglass doors, light inner fenders) 3,510 lbs. (without fiberglass doors, light inner fenders)

The #824 1963-1/2 lightweight Galaxie of Dick Brannan.

The interior of the Galaxie sports only the necessary items for racing including a tach, oil pressure gauge, and floor shifter. The radio and heater were deleted at the factory.

Ford technicians, accomplished the task in the Ford Experimental Garage in Dearborn during December 1962. The car served as a test vehicle until the new models arrived.

In 1963, the engine moved up 21 cubic inches to the familiar 427 figure and both the 427 High-and Low-Riser engines had twin four-barrel carburetor set-ups and again came with the 4.11-geared differential. The High-Risers usually competed in the Super/ Stock while the Low-Riser engine was usually associated with A/Stock.

Ford statistical expert Greg Donohue indicated that he thought that there were actually 212 of these cars built and estimated there is a high percentage of them, at least 150, still remaining.

The new '63 -1/2s were introduced at the NHRA Winter Nationals where, because they were so new, they began competing in the Limited Production/ Factory Experimental class. Soon they were allowed to compete in Super Stock.

These second-year lightweights performed well with drivers Bill Lawton, Phil Bonner, Les Ritchey, and Gas Ronda all scoring many victories. Brannan stuck with his test car (#823) and set 22 track records with 65 victories.

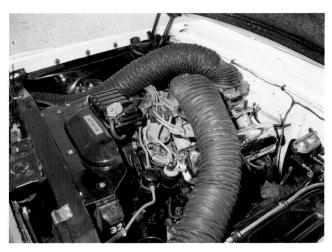

The 1963-1/2 Galaxie's ducting originated from the void of the removed high beam headlights. Air went directly into the carburetors. The idea was used on Thunderbolt in 1964.

His was the first Ford ever to set an NHRA record in Super Stock class.

1964 Galaxie Lightweights

The 1964 Lightweights reverted to a fiberglass hood with a bubble similar to the Thunderbolts. The use of aluminum and fiberglass was limited. The

The Brannan car has been restored and represents one of the most-successful lightweight Galaxies.

Lightweight car fan Jim Frigge replicated a 1963-1/2 Galaxie and it's very close to the real thing, including the period 427 engine.

cars now came with steel fenders and trunk lid. The production 1964 Galaxie 500 two-door hardtop was already lighter than the 1963 version—at 3,582 lbs. versus 3,620 lbs. In the Lightweight, all the deadening material was again removed. Better weight transfer, a big issue during the 1963 drag racing season, meant the battery was now relocated to the trunk.

The 1964 version saw the initial introduction of the awesome 427 High-Riser 427 engine equipped with tubular headers. Reportedly, the engine was capable of providing about 100 additional horsepower, pushing it well over 500 horsepower. It also featured fiberglass ducts funneling cool air from the grille to the air cleaner.

The engines included high dome pistons and a new design for the combustion chambers. What really got attention was that using company specs, the engine compression ratio could be raised as high as 14 to 1. The redesigned cylinder heads

The Courtesy Ford Thunderbolt in 1960s racing action.

Bob Plumer

A 1964 Galaxie fastback makes its way to the drag race starting line.

incorporated larger ports along with 1.73-inch exhausts and 2.19-inch intakes. Sitting atop the monster engine were a pair of huge 780-cfm Holley carburetors.

Of the 50 1964 Lightweight Galaxies that were constructed, 25 of them were equipped with Lincoln automatic transmissions while the remaining 25 had Ford "Toploader" manual 4-speed units. Most of the '64 Lightweights in the NHRA Stock Classes were much more competitive.

Former Galaxie driver Skip Norman explained that many of the drivers of these Ford Galaxie Lightweights modified their cars on their own to increase performance.

"They installed traction bars and custom engine headers," he explained. He also added that these cars ran in both the Super Stock and A/FX Classes. He added that NHRA required seven-inch tires in Super Stock and allowed 10-inchers in the A/FX Class.

Fairlane Lightweights
The Thunderbolts

Ford introduced something else in 1964 that put the Galaxies to shame. Basically it involved equipping the 1964 mid-sized Fairlane with the powerful 427 engine.

Even the stylish 1964 Galaxie 500XL had a performance look about it.

The story actually started in 1963 when performance Ford dealer, Bob Tasca, owner of Tasca Ford, installed a 427 mill into a 1963 Fairlane 500 two-door hardtop. The successful car got the eyes and ears of Ford brass.

The company was unable to install the physically larger 427 engine during the normal production line process. Ford again struck an agreement with Dearborn Steel Tubing and the rest is history. Just over 100 Thunderbolts were produced. They were built from scratch to compete in Super Stock class. Ford initially produced only 10 maroon manual 4-speed Thunderbolts and one automatic version.

The NHRA balked and said a minimum of at least 50 with each transmission had to be produced to qualify for the class. They would have to run A/FX until production numbers could be documented. After satisfying the NHRA rule makers, the cars were allowed in Super Stock competition by February 1964.

Thunderbolts were built in three groups, with Group one (completed in October 1963) was the first 11 cars. These were all painted burgundy with 10 of them equipped with manual four-speed transmissions and one with an automatic. The first T-Bolts went to the top Ford drivers including Dick Brannan, Gas Ronda, Les Ritchey, Bill Lawton, Phil Bonner, Butch Leal and Mickey Thompson, Len Richter, Paul Harvey, Clester Andrews, and Don Turner.

Group two consisted of 39 cars, all white, with nine four-speeds and 30 automatics. They were produced between December 1963 and February 1964. The third group consisted of at least 50 cars produced between March and May of 1964. There have been reports that as many as 127 Thunderbolts could have been built. Some dealers may have contracted with Dearborn Steel directly after formal production ceased.

The initial 11 Thunderbolts were delivered in late 1963 at the Ford Test Track in Dearborn, Michigan, and later were tested at the Ford Proving Ground in Kingman, Arizona, on the way to the Winter Nationals in Pomona, California. Dick Brannan and all Ford Team members were elated when they found the new Thunderbolts actually came in under the 3,200-pound limit. That meant fuel could be used as ballast to meet the required limit.

The Thunderbolts were all Fairlane 500 two-door models and could be differentiated by their serial number. They came without creature comforts like a radio, heater, undersealing, sound deadener, body insulation, rear window cranks, carpeting, armrests, sun visors, spare tire and jack, and windshield wipers.

Fiberglass body parts were used throughout during construction of these cars. For a Factory Drag Team member or first time racer, the cars were really special.

This #823 1963 Galaxie was an NHRA Super Stock record holder.

Above: *Some Thunderbolts used considerable fiberglass in the body, including the front bumper.*

Left: *The most recognizable item on the Thunderbolt was the large, bulbous reverse scoop that monopolized the hood.*

Three or four of the Group One cars could be considered as the prototype versions and at first were equipped with a cloverleaf hood and fiberglass front bumper. Plexiglass replaced the window glass. Capable of running in the mid-11s, the cars carried no warranty and had to be picked up at the Dearborn location.

Even though these Fairlane 500-based cars were classified in groups, they were not identical with deviations in fiberglass and other materials. Some of the early Thunderbolts used fiberglass bumpers, but later all changed to aluminum to meet NHRA specs. Some of the cars had front-mounted tow hooks while

others did not. All the cars had some type of cutting on the rear quarters for rear tire clearance.

Traction bars were incorporated in their design to prevent body roll and improve down force. The cars came with square bars welded to the rear axle housing stretching forward to a cross member that was also used as a drive shaft safety loop. It wasn't surprising to see these bars lengthened and some even were stretched forward all the way to the firewall.

Under the hood sat the ultimate power plant. The cars had a center-oiler, 427 high-riser configuration with the expected twin four-barrel

1964 Mickey Thompson Thunderbolt	
Engine:	Ford 427 cid V-8
Horsepower:	Rated hp: 425 (Actual hp: 500+)
Transmission:	Borg-Warner-built 4-speed manual with Hurst shifter
Chassis:	Includes extra crossmembers, radius rods and modified leaf springs.
Weight:	3,228 lbs. (with full tank)
Top Speed:	124.88 mph (11.61-second quarter mile)
Miscellaneous:	One of the first 11 produced.

Holley carburetors. They came with unique dual fresh air intake tubing that was made possible through removal of the inboard headlights. That funneled cool air directly to the intake.

The intake manifold had higher intake ports raising the carburetors enough to require a bubble in the hood. In order to fit the larger 427 engine into the Fairlane, it was necessary to rework the shock and spring towers for header clearance. The engines were reportedly capable of over 500 horsepower at well over 7,000 rpm.

Author/photographer Mike Mueller says Thunderbolt number 10 was an experiment. Sold to

Mickey Thompson for $1, it used copies of Chrysler Hemi heads that were drilled to fit the Ford 427 block. Disappointed with the outcome. Ford took back the engine in the summer of 1964 and gave the car to Jess Tyree. It was restored in 1990.

The T-10 four-speed transmission had a lightweight aluminum case coupled to the standard 4.44 rear axle assembly. Like the Galaxie Lightweights, the Lincoln name came on-board again with the three-speed automatic equipped cars. A special bell housing was required and the transmission had the kick-down capability removed so it had to be moved manually through each gear. The rear axle assembly was similar to the four-speed cars but a 4.57 ratio was used.

A typical car set-up might include a three-leaf spring on the right rear, with a two-leaf spring on the left rear. The 125-pound diesel truck battery was mounted in the trunk, directly over the right rear tire.

The Thunderbolts competed well against the vaunted MOPAR competition. At the 1964 Winternationals, Butch Leal blew away the MOPARs in the Super Stock Class. He ran a 12.05 elapsed time at 120.16 mph during his final victory run. Later in the season, he made an 11.47-second run. Leal also took the US Fuel and Gas Championships at Bakersfield, California. Gas Ronda took the NHRA Top Stock Championship.

Mike Doherty described Gas (full name Gaspar) Ronda's successful run this way in 1968:

This excellent recreation of the Don Nicholson Thunderbolt receives great attention everytime it is displayed.

The engine for the 1967 lightweight Fairlane was a single four-barrel 427 V-8.

"Gas' quick clutch cut Leal's similar T-bolt in a close HRM semi-final 12.04 to 12.10, and he met Detroiter Al Eckstrand. His Ford... simply outran the Mopar, consistent at 12.08-119.68 to Lawman's 12.21-114."

Doherty added that part of the winnings for Ronda was a new Barracuda that was displayed at the Davis Ford dealership with a sign that read "I won it in a Ford."

During the 1965 model year, Ford produced no lightweight cars for the various stock classes.

1966 427 Lightweight Fairlanes

They definitely weren't Thunderbolts, but don't downgrade the performance of these 1966 427 Fairlanes. Only 57 were built and carried a lightweight lift-off fiberglass hood with an integrated functional scoop. Also, all the sound-deadening material was removed and there was that ever-familiar set of 427 identifier tags on the front fenders.

There was a pair of the 427 high-rise mills, the W Code with a single four-barrel carb and the R Code engine with a pair of them. The resulting horsepower figures were 410 and 425, respectively.

The R-Code versions also produced a stump-pulling 4,380 pounds-feet of torque. All but eight of models built carried that more-powerful R Code.

Judging from the equipment it carried the model definitely had the strong hint of a racing machine. There was a special heavy-duty rear axle, custom race-type shocks, and front wheel disc brakes.

1967 427 Lightweight Fairlanes

The Ford version of the lightweight concept was continued during the 1967 model year when 60 427 Fairlanes were built with the Lightweight Drag Package. The parts and pieces used in the package were identical to those offered in the 1966 package.

As was also the case with the previous year, only eight of the single four-barrel carb versions existed. Yet one of those W Ford models was a significant performer, winning both the 1969 and 1970 NHRA Winter Nationals. The Fairlane's best effort was a 10.90 second run at 126 mph. That stellar performance was the record for two years.

Former car owner Bob Russell explained the Fairlane Lightweight initially came with a steel hood, but the first buyer was assured of a fiberglass hood when it was available.

Interestingly, 1967 was also a great year for the 427 Fairlane as it ran on the NASCAR oval tracks. The Fairlanes prepared in stock car trim took the checkered flags at both the Daytona 500 and Riverside 500 with Mario Andretti and Parnelli Jones at the wheel.

BOB TASCA'S
Fantastic Fords

Bob Tasca had a dream about promoting his Ford dealership through drag racing. He wasn't the first one to make the connection.

Ace Wilson had the same idea with his Pontiac dealership in Michigan as did the Sachs and Sons Mercury dealership and Russ Davis Ford—all active drag racing car sponsors. Norm Kraus of Chicago was an influential Dodge performance car entrepreneur and was active in drag racing circles through his Grand Spaulding Dodge.

Tasca Ford became an icon in drag racing history and Bob Tasca became a major influence from his Ford dealership at 777 Taunton Avenue in East Providence, Rhode Island. In 1968, Bob Tasca told *Super Stock* magazine his philosophy of racing and selling cars.

"Make the car fast first, then put your name on it and put it in the showroom as often as you can."

After nearly a decade selling Fords, including several special editions, Bob Tasca became interested in racing them in 1961. He told author Mike Mueller his interest came from some competitive Chevrolets.

"I was losing business to Chevrolet because we weren't equal to them in performance," he recalled.

Young driver Bill Lawton kept bragging about his Chevy drag racing exploits and Tasca was determined to show that a Ford could do just as well.

Tasca mechanics prepared a 1962 Galaxie with a 406-cid V-8. Lawton was shocked when mechanic John Healey beat Lawton's best Chevy time out of the box with the Tasca-prepared Ford. It ran in 13.33 seconds in April 1962 at the Charleston, Rhode Island, Dragway.

Lawton turned to Fords with a similar Tasca-prepared 1962 Galaxie and stayed with them until his driving career ended in 1971.

Bob Tasca and his crew also were visionaries about Ford Motor Company's involvement in drag racing. In 1962, Tasca took a new mid-sized

The Tasca Ford Thunderbolt as it looks today.

Fairlane and stuffed it with a 406-cid V-8. Some special body and chassis prep was done with the help of Detroit Steel and Tubing.

The result was the "Challenger," a Tasca creation that aroused interest around the country and resulted in 100 Fairlanes being built in 1964 with Ford's hefty 427-cid V-8. Lawton drove a version called the Zimmy II to national records. The "Challenger" foreshadowed Ford's own Thunderbolt lightweight production drag racers.

When the Mustang premiered in April 1964, the Tasca crew thought of its drag racing potential. By 1965, they were preparing the Zimmy III, a Mustang with Ford's SOHC 427-cid engine under its hood. The car won the Winternationals, NASCAR Nationals and also captured the first Super Stock Nationals—all with Bill Lawton at the wheel.

While Ford was building hefty engines for drag racing and NASCAR use, average Ford buyers often had a hard time accessing them. Tasca's team decided to take things into their own hands.

They took a Ford Police Interceptor V-8, put it in a Mustang and created a car that could do a 13- second quarter mile in street dress. They also produced the Mystery Mustang in 1966, a match-race car with an altered wheelbase, built in conjunction with the famed Holman-Moody expertise.

Tasca Ford promoted the popular Mustang as the KR-8 or "King of the Road." It was a hit for Tasca but Ford Motor Company executives balked at producing this kind of Mustang.

Then *Hot Rod* editor Eric Dahlquist, who liked the car, decided to promote it with readers and published a poll in the magazine. Agreeable readers obliged and flooded Dearborn offices with mail that asked for the Tasca-concept Mustang. Ford execs took another look.

The result was the legendary Cobra Jet Ford engine that premiered in 1968, including a Mustang version. Just to emphasize the point, 50 lightweight Ford 428 CJ Mustangs were crafted in the factory and became winners that season guided by the likes of Hubert Platt and Don Nicholson.

The car became a legend among a legion of Mustang owners and was a strong seller for Ford.

Tasca also sold John Force one of his first Ford racing machines. Force became one of the top drivers in NHRA history.

Bob Tasca was inducted in the Motorsports Hall of Fame and wrote a book called "You Will Be Satisfied" that now is used as a college textbook.

Satisfaction was a key reason many buyers returned over and over to Tasca's Ford and Lincoln-Mercury dealerships.

Tasca told *Mustang Illustrated* in 1992 drag racing was a good way to do business but he told Ford executives he wasn't interested in what he called "image" racing efforts at Daytona or Indianapolis.

Bill Lawton and the Tasca Ford Mustang were featured in a 1967 Crane Cam ad.

"When I could sell what I raced, I raced it. If I couldn't sell it, I wasn't interested. I can make money drag racing because it's mainstream."

The Tasca Ford dealership continues to win quality awards from the Ford Motor Company.

When many people think of Fords and drag racing, Tasca is the name that also comes to mind. The dealership has achieved Bob Tasca's goal and much more.

The Tasca Ford dealership's Mustang going away in 1966 action.

Falcon Lightweights

1964-'65 427 Falcon A/FX Lightweights

Even the most-avid vintage drag racing fan might forget that there were also Lightweight Falcons during the mid-1960s. The reason they're so hard to remember is there were only two such factory-sponsored lightweight machines constructed.

But when you hear who the drivers were, you will understand the significance of these machines. Dick Brannan and Phil Bonner were the recipients, and it didn't get much better than that.

The Bonner Falcon really wasn't planned, Brannan explained.

"After getting word that Ford was building such a Falcon-based vehicle, Phil bought and started construction on his own Falcon down in Georgia. Because of safety concerns, it was decided that the car should be completed by the company and it was later transferred to Dearborn Steel where it was completed. That accounts for the second 427 powered Falcon that year."

The Falcon Lightweights also were built by Dearborn Steel Tubing. Ford's Special Vehicles Division and DST took Ford's lightest model (the Falcon) and the most powerful engine (the 427) and combined them to form this potent machine. Not as much weight reduction was required since the Falcons were already very light.

The 1964 production Galaxie 500 XL two-door hardtop weighed in at 3,622 pounds while the production Fairlane two-door hardtop carried 2,678

pounds. The production version of the 1964 Falcon two-door hardtop was just 2,545 pounds.

DST stripped just about everything. The metal front bumper, doors, hood and fenders were all replaced with fiberglass replicas. As this was a smaller vehicle, it was necessary to bulge the rear quarters in order to accommodate the wider rear slicks.

A new material, Lucite, replaced the factory glass, greatly improving weight reduction. The cars also had a pair of lightweight bucket seats replacing the heavier factory production seats. Surprisingly, the complete factory dashboard was retained.

The Falcons had basically the identical 427 engine used in the Thunderbolts and that included an aluminum Borg-Warner four-speed and a 4.57 Locker rear axle assembly.

Another Falcon Lightweight gained national attention. It was the Rankin Ford sponsored "Wild Child" driven by Ev Rouse. The non-factory Falcon was powered by a small block 289-cubic inch mill, and competed in match races against the best racers in the country. With its small block engine, the "Child" had to compete in the B/FX class. The car was capable of 11-second, 117-mile per hour performance in the quarter mile.

1965 NHRA Ultra Stock Lightweight Falcon

There was also a Lightweight one-off Falcon that was driven by Dave Lyall, a shop employee at Bob Ford. Initially, it was a fiberglass creation used by Ford Styling to introduce the new 1964 Falcon body.

Dave Lyall was later given the body and it was immediately sent to DST for its conversion

Dick Brannan poses with his 427 High-Rise 1964 Falcon. This was the first of only two officially built by Ford.

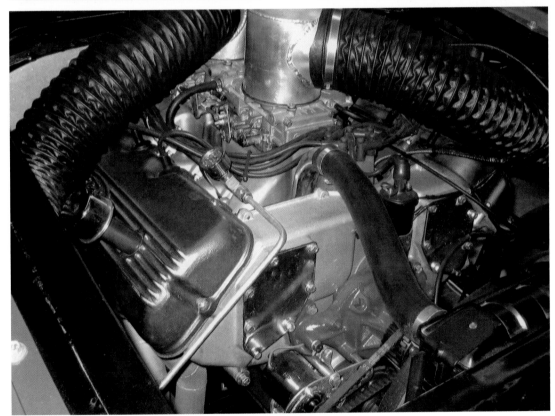

Above: *The "Wild Child" Falcon drag car was a prominent Canadian lightweight from London, Ontario, that participated in many U. S. races.*
Joe Germann

Left: *That's 427 Ford power under the hood of the "Wild Child" Falcon lightweight.*
Joe Germann

magic. It was equipped with an SOHC 427 engine and weighed under 3,000 pounds. Lyall's "Quartermaster" vehicle did its thing in the Ultra Stock NHRA Class with a time of 9.80 seconds.

Lightweight Mustangs

During the last half of the 1960s decade, a number of Factory Lightweight Mustangs deviations appeared. They varied from Factory Experimental to Funny Cars to the 1968-1/2 Cobra Jet Mustangs.

1965 A/FX Mustangs

These machines were bad to the bone! In fact, a 2004 track test by *Musclecar Review Magazine* of all the early A/FX cars showed a 1965 Mustang A/FX was easily the fastest with a 10.90- second, 130.16 mph clocking.

The power plant was the brand new 427 (Single Overhead Cam) SOHC "Cammer" engine capable of a spellbinding 660 horsepower. The increase in

This was the first 1966 427 altered wheelbase SOHC Mustang the first to be equipped with fuel injection and an automatic transmission.

performance was attributed to the ability of the engine to spin at a higher rpm and breathe better while doing so

In 1966 the Hilborn Fuel Injected version could run on gasoline, alcohol or a high percentage of nitro methane and alcohol. The new radical design had larger, lighter valves, an improved intake manifold, two 715-cfm Holley four-barrels and a single camshaft without pushrods on each cylinder head.

Ford built a total of 12 standard wheelbase SOHC powered 427 Mustangs for 1965. The first two 427 Mustangs were built by Dearborn Steel Tubing while the 10 remaining cars were built by Holman and Moody at Charlotte, North Carolina. Only five of the 12 cars were equipped with the SOHC engine. The remainder received the 427-cid pushrod engine. These cars were similar again to the Thunderbolts using fiberglass components and steel bodies.

To allow for the large and heavy engine, the entire spring tower assembly was removed and replaced with a unique "Twist Leaf" arrangement that worked like a torsion bar system. This made room for the engine and reduced weight.

These Mustangs went to a who's-who of Ford drivers including Bill Lawton, Dick Brannan, Phil Bonner, Les Ritchey, and Gas Ronda.

Testing continued and with Brannan and his supervisor Charlie Gray happy with the changes, the SOHC Mustangs started to appear. With Ford's drag racing success stories there soon was a rumor that some well-known Chrysler teams were scrambling and the Mopar products were starting to show up with acid-dipped steel bodies, altered wheelbases, all with the goal of weighing less than the Ford Mustangs.

Ford decided it would build one special Lightweight SOHC Mustang. It had an altered

Besides Thunderbolts, legendary driver Hubert Platt also drove an A/FX Mustang. This replica illustrates the famous car very accurately.

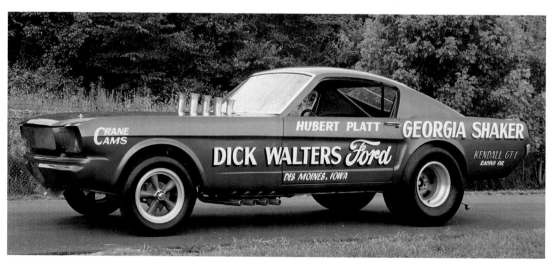

The 1966 "Daddy Warbucks" Mustang featured tall intake stacks protruding through the hood.

wheelbase and a target weight of about 2,700 pounds. The car was to be built in secrecy with the help of Holman/Moody fabricator Eddy Pagan.

Everything about the car was completely different including the altered wheelbase, engine set-back, lots of fiberglass and aluminum, a complete roll cage and an aviation-type seat. When the car was completed, Brannan was at the wheel, and the new Mustang was runner up at the NHRA Summer Nationals, but the SOHC engine blew a head gasket in the final round. The car won the AHRA "World Championship" and the year end "Factory

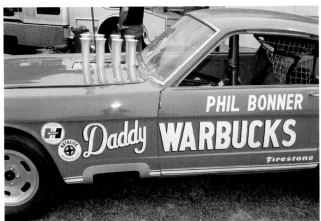

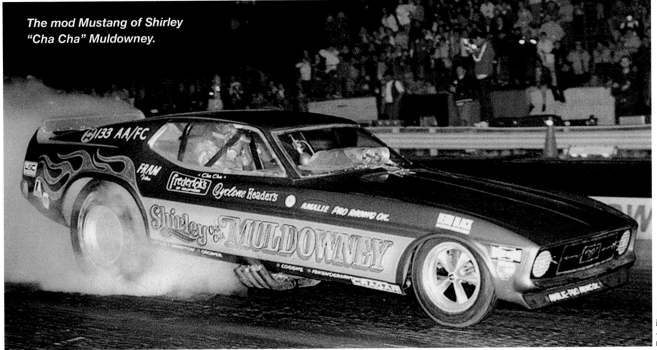

The mod Mustang of Shirley "Cha Cha" Muldowney.

Bob Plumer

Phil Bonner in the "Warbucks" A/FX Mustang and sponsored by Archway Ford.

Bob Plumer

Showdown." It never lost a race for the remainder of the 1965 season.

The Paul Norris 1965 A/FX Fastback (one of the 12) was another Holman/ Moody conversion that served as a Ford test car. A 427 SOHC was in place and the wheel openings were each moved about three inches forward.

Another famous 1965 Mustang A/FX fastback was the Bob Ford-sponsored car driven by "Dyno Don" Nicholson in the late 1960s. It was highly successful in NHRA competition, holding world records for a number of years during the period. A number of other noted drivers wheeled the machine, including Hubert Platt, Len Richter, and Jerry Harvey.

That particular car was located and restored by Curt Vogt. The gold and blue A/FX Mustang was sponsored by the Bob Ford Dealership of Dearborn, Michigan.

The "MR 4-SPEED" 1965 A/FX Mustang was another outstanding performer (with Clester Andrews at the wheel). Much of its success occurred competing in AHRA events. Its best E.T. was an impressive 10.47 seconds.

1966 A/FX Mustangs

The "Funny Car" terminology really fit when referring to the front clip of some later model and rare Mustangs. After extensive research, it was decided to stretch the wheelbase just forward of the windshield about 10 inches. The name "Long Nose Mustang" came to be sometime in 1966. These cars came with the same front and rear suspension that the '65 A/FX Mustangs used, but it worked much better because of the engine set-back and longer wheelbase.

Ronda explained that NHRA didn't have a class for these "Funny Cars" so they were put in the C

This famous 1965 A/FX Mustang, driven by Clester Andrews, was sponsored by Wickersham Ford of Orange, Texas.

Two big names in mid-1960s A/FX Mustang racing were Russ Davis Ford and the immortal Gas Ronda.

Fuel Class where they blew the competition away. With Ronda at the wheel, the machine competed extensively in special match racing events. As more of the cars showed up, a Funny Car Class was initiated.

Gas drove the car in late 1966 and 1967. During the 1966 season, the drag fans and track owners demanded the door slammers go faster and faster. Ford contracted Holman and Moody to build "The biggest, fastest Mustangs they could construct," said Gas Ronda.

They started with a couple sticks of 2 x 3 inch-square tubing and built a complete fiberglass body. A change was made to the front clip where approximately 16 inches was added just forward of the windshield.

The cars continued to use the same 1965 Mustang rear suspension and with the engine set back 15 inches, handling continued to improve.

Mustang drag car collector Brent Hajek explained, "The stretched cars started out with the new C-6 automatic and worked quite well with the fuel injected, Nitro burning SOHC engine." Hajek has re-created the Ronda car and exhibits it occasionally.

The hitters that got the cars were Bill Lawton, Brannan, Bonner, Tommy Grove, Darrell Droke, and Ronda. And believe it, these guys went out

and changed the drag racing scene forever.

Phil Bonner's "Daddy Warbucks" 1966 Mustang was one of the most remembered machines. With its neat name, how could it not be remembered? Unfortunately, the car was wrecked during a race and not repaired for the remaining season.

Post-A/FX Mustang

In 1967, the altered Mustangs fell out of favor. Ford no longer budgeted these cars, so the teams continued to use their 1966 models. There was some minor support with engines and transmissions, but gone were the days of seemingly endless factory support.

Ford thought it made sense to concentrate on improving production car performance and image. That could have been one reason the company developed the special Cobra Jet Mustang Drag Cars.

Ford's corporate executives approved one specially designed Mustang and it was quickly dubbed the "Super Mustang." Brannan, in addition to his factory driver activity, was asked to be involved with the project along with Chuck Foulger.

Tom "The Mongoose" McEwen was selected to drive the special project car. While the exciting concept "Super Mustang" drew a lot of attention, it never entered NHRA competition.

A modern rendition of the 1968 Cobra Jet is this 427-powered version.

1968 Cobra Jet Drag Mustangs

To any Mustang drag racing fans, the serial numbers told the story on 50 specially built fastback Cobra Jet Mustangs that were constructed in the latter part of the model year. The identifying numbers were 1355007 to 1355056. Yep, they were Cobra Jets, but there was a lot more to them than their street brothers. These 50 cars were screamers. The model was so popular the company built 400 more civilized versions for public consumption.

Initially, there were 11-14 Super Stock Eliminator drag versions built by Holman-Moody, eight of which competed at the 1968 Winternationals. With a 428 Cobra Jet Wedge engine for power, the new Cobra Jet Mustangs quickly showed their class.

As usual, the drivers who got these initial haulers again included the best Ford had to offer with the likes of Nicholson, Ronda, Platt, Jerry Harvey, Al Joniec, and Bill Ireland. The remainder of the fleet was campaigned by performance Ford dealerships that were involved in drag racing.

The factory versions were to run in the Super Stock/E Automatic Class, while the remainder ran in the Super Stock Eliminator Class. Hubert Platt actually had one of each.

The engine bay was programmed to receive a 390 mill, but each car received a 428 Cobra Jet engine. There would also be a heavy-duty four-speed transmission and rear end. Wide oval tires, staggered rear shocks and a fresh air induction package were installed.

"Ohio George" Montgomery drove the "Mr. Gasket" drag racer.

There was no significant weight reduction done to the Cobra Jet drag cars. They carried factory sheet metal and none of the expected aluminum or fiberglass body panels were used. Some minor weight reduction efforts were done. The car was already light and fit well into the NHRA Super Stock class due to conservative factoring related to engine horsepower.

The oft-involved Tasca Ford Dealership had earlier proved the concept when they modified a small number of 1967 Mustangs with Police Interceptor 428s and installed 1963 Low Riser 427 cylinder heads. Tasca Ford driver Bill Lawton was so impressed with the dealer-built creation that he said it was "faster than a jet." Reportedly, that's where the Cobra Jet name came from.

Ford quickly showed it had a real winner with its new Mustang as it won the SS/E class at the nationals with Al Joniec taking the victory in 11.49 seconds at 120.6 mph. Even more impressive was that the opposition was another Cobra Jet, driven by Hubert Platt.

One 1968 Cobra Jet team that certainly deserved attention was the Canadian-based Sandy Elliot team. Driver Barrie Poole set a Canadian class record with an 11.87 elapsed time. He did even better when he crossed the border and made an 11.32 run. The Elliot drag cars were recognizable with their peppermint striping on the back half of the car.

These Mustangs would go on to win consistently for many years into the future. The former Nicholson / Dick Brannan car competed during the latter part of the 1960s and earned a number of NHRA Division IV titles. With some modifications, the car got into the low 11s at close to 125 mph. Ford was so impressed it provided a little factory help until 1970 when the company backed out of racing.

Gasser Lightweight Mustangs

"Ohio George" Montgomery was one of the most famous Gasser drag racers. His legend grew during the middle 1960s driving his SOHC-powered Malco AA/Gas supercharged Willys. But Ford wanted to use his success in a stock car-bodied Gasser. In 1967, a lightweight fiberglass body simulating a new fastback Mustang was installed on one of his tube frame chassis. It would be the first time that a factory-bodied car competed in the Gasser class.

It made no difference to Montgomery, who kept on setting NHRA records, including winning the Super

A Cyclone Automotive ad featured the Malco Gasser Mustang of "Ohio George" Montgomery.

Eliminator Class at the Spring Nationals, cutting an 8.73 elapsed time at 162.74 mph.

Boss 429 Mustang Lightweights

In 1969, another fiberglass Mustang was made available to Montgomery, equipped with twin-turbochargers feeding a "Boss 429" power plant! The 1969 "Mr. Gasket" Mustang entry was a top-gun machine and won just about everything out there. That same year, Ford (with Kar Kraft modification and assistance) came out with half a dozen lightened Boss 429 Mustangs.

Most of the weight reduction came from deleting the sound deadener and adding super-light magnesium wheels plus a factory aluminum radiator/water pump. Ford called the weight reductions its "Super Stock Lightweight Package." These cars carried the Ford C6 transmission and Detroit Locker rear ends.

Reportedly, the cars were capable of 11-second quarter mile performance. Brent Hajek claims to have found one of these cars and restored it to its late-1960s configuration. This is one of the six built, and was campaigned by Tasca Ford who wanted the fastest street car in the country. According to John Healy, who worked at Tasca, after a few engine and suspension changes, they got the car into the low 11's on street tires. Montgomery continued to run his car until 1974.

Chapter 5

MERCURY
LIGHTWEIGHTS

By 1964, the Super Stock Classes of NHRA and AHRA, and IHRA had the attention of the avid drag fans. The Mercury Division of Ford proved to be one of the most aggressive even though it spent much less money than the Ford Division.

With its two US directors in Frank Hernandez and Al Turner, and John Phillips in Canada, Mercury did its thing in the Factory Experimental Class. Again, the heavy hitters were in place, with drivers Don Nicholson, Ed Schartman, and Jack Chrisman the top runners with the Mercury Division machines.

It was the small Comet that was almost exclusively used in the Super Stock Classes, and for a time it was the king of the hill. There were two versions of the Comet Factory Experimental models, the A/FX and B/FX, the only basic difference being the large and small block power plants that they carried. There was also a weight difference with the A/FX cars coming in at about 3,240 pounds, while the B/FXers came in at only 2,600 pounds.

The NHRA didn't allow supercharging and altered wheelbases, but that didn't keep the best teams from equipping their Mercury products with those attributes to run at match races. Having top drivers with their cars so equipped brought out huge crowds wherever they appeared.

Dyno Don Nicholson's Comet in racing action.

Bob Plumer

Another Comet driver in 1964 was Ronnie Sox, later of Sox and Martin Plymouth fame.

Phil Hall Collection

It got to the point that it was necessary to have two cars, one for Super Stock racing in NHRA and the other for match racing. Those match racers were the first "Funny Car" design that has evolved into the 330-mile-per-hour screamers of today.

1964 A/FX and B/FX Comets

The first year of lightweight A/FX racing for Mercury was 1964 when 11 Comets were constructed. All but one were coupes. The final version was a station wagon.

These cars were definitely Lightweights of the first order and were modified by the Bill Stroppe organization. Fiberglass was used in a manner similar to the way it had been used in the 1964 Thunderbolt. The fiberglass was used for the hood, fenders (front only), bumpers and doors. Even the front wheels were lighter because they were fabricated from magnesium rather than steel.

Plexiglass reportedly was used in place of the window glass to bring the weight down even further. The radiator, intended for a six-cylinder engine application, was in place.

This was a Mercury, so there was the Mercury engine, right? Well, it did say "Mercury Super

Both the Nicholson A/FX coupe and station wagon were sponsored by the Atlanta District Mercury Dealers.

This 1964 Comet clone is close to the look of the original with the exception of the modern scoop and wide rear slicks.

Marauder" on the valve covers, but the truth was it was that old reliable dual-carb Ford 427 High Riser, reportedly capable of over 500 horsepower.

It was the ultimate cut and paste squeeze job to drop that giant mill into place. The nifty twin hood scoops on the forward hood provided cool air directly into the twin carburetors. They were reportedly more effective than the headlight intake style used on the Thunderbolt.

A number of the A/FX cars would receive the powerful SOHC Cammer 427 engine, a new high-technology engine that was worth more than 600 horsepower.

The remainder of the engine was pure-racer with a Ford four-speed tranny and a Galaxie driveshaft. Clearly visible were the large traction bars that really set off the rear end of the cars. However, the cars did not come from the factory with the bars installed. That installation work was done by the teams.

Even though these unique cars carried the "Experimental" connotation, there were NO significant altered wheelbase implications. Besides the racy bubble hood and slightly rearward body rake, these cars didn't appear to be that far from stock, that is until they were put on the drag strip.

This 1964 "Comet Cyclone" C/FX lightweight carries a 289-cubic inch small block V-8.

The magnificent collection of Brent Hajek contains two prime examples of these cars, both of the Don Nicholson cars, his coupe and station wagon. Both machines were white with crossed flags on the sides. The sponsor was the "Atlanta District Mercury Dealers" in bold letters on the sides. Crane Cams and Jardine Headers were also noted as sponsors on the car.

The station wagon had the expected 427 Hi-Riser engine and four-speed transmission. The rear end gear ratio was 4.56. Hajek indicated the wagon does

Performance, competition, and the Comet really went together during the 1960s, as typified by the car's checkered flag emblem.

not have the Plexiglass that was reportedly used on all these A/FX racers.

Nicholson had a best estimated time of 10.55 seconds in the car. It was actually his first Ford race car. He took delivery of the machine in November 1963 and kept it on the track until April 1964. He then received his Comet coupe and finished the NHRA season with it. The wagon was then passed on to Ed Schartman who campaigned the car the remainder of the season.

Nicholson's coupe was similar to the wagon in the way it was equipped, except it also had a fiberglass rear deck and the advertised Plexiglass windows. With Nicholson at the wheel, it showed a best estimated time of 10.65 seconds. It was one of the most successful drag cars in history, with 78 wins and only a single loss during the 1964 season.

It is reported that there was a limited production of the 1964 B/FX Comets accomplished with Bill Stroppe involved. Not all were up to manhandling the A/FX type of power under the hood, so a B/FX with a potent 289 small block under the hood was the answer.

But on the match-racing scene, where just about everything went, and when nitro fuel was combined

Below Left: The "Ugly Duckling" represented the '64 A/FX Mercury Comet station wagon of Don Nicholson that ran in 1963 and 1964.

Below Right: The similarly painted A/FX coupe had 78 wins in 79 races during the 1964 season. The coupe held a national NHRA record of 11.05 seconds.

The SOHC 427 engine was the muscle for the A/FX Mercurys. This one was the engine for Hayden Proffitt's machine.

with a supercharger, look out! Jack Chrisman in the "Sachs & Sons" A/FX Comet with a 6.71 15 percent overdriven blower demonstrated a boiling 156 mph top speed and 10.13 clocking in the quarter mile. During the season, it earned the title of "The World's Fastest Accelerating Stock Bodied Car." These blown A/FX machines were described as "absolutely scary" by those that saw them run.

A *Hot Rod* profile of the Chrisman / Sachs and Sons Comet in the September issue included information about pieces added to the car but said Chrisman had tried to use as much stock equipment as possible. The article noted "fiberglass abounds." The photos showed such touches as the blown engine, Doug's exhausts—a mad pipe organ arrangement—an explosion-proof

This B/FX Comet is sponsored by Cerullo Motors, Cometland U.S.A., Depew, New York. Many dealers backed lightweight drag cars in the 1960s.

bell housing shield, traction bars and the single racing bucket inside.

"Whatever the outcome," concluded writer Earl Dahlquist, "the machine will generate unprecedented interest when it runs. Drag racing may never be the same."

1965 A/FX and B/FX Comets

The best information on the '65 A/FX Comets is that only six factory machines were built, but reportedly there was an additional version built as a factory backup and sold to a Maryland Mercury dealer. It's not known exactly how many of this design would be copied and homemade versions made, but there were definitely some of them on the scene.

These outlandish machines were killers at the national drag strips, saying good-bye to the lightweight Dodges, Pontiacs, and Chevys of the era. Of the six cars built, four carried the SOHC 427 while the final two were equipped with the Medium-Riser 427.

All six A/FXers went to top-gun drivers like Arnie Beswick, Hayden Proffitt, Eddie Schartman, Don Nicholson, and George Delorean. Lightweight fans will tell you that the number actually may be seven as Don Nicholson also wheeled a 1965 A/FX Comet— at least it sure looked like one.

That's an interesting story. Nicholson created his "look-alike" '65 by starting with a 1964 Comet A/FX and using a 1965 front clip and rear quarter panels to produce a "65." Also, his Comet was powered by a blown SOHC engine. The car was very familiar being a bright red in color with gold lettering on the sides announcing it was a "Comet Cyclone."

Above: The B/FX engine carries a pair of four-barrel carbs, rather than the single- carb version used in the C/FX cars.

Right: This 1965 A/FX clone is owned by John Gotshall and is detailed similarly to Don Nicholson's famous Comet.

The 1965 A/FX Comet pictured was driven by Hayden Proffitt originally. It was restored by John Gotshall.

The '65 factory cars carried the fiberglass front and steel rear bumpers, fiberglass fenders, ram air hood, along with fiberglass doors and deck lid. In addition, there was a three-point cage installed over the driver. The Ford top-loader four-speed tranny continued to be the favorite unit with these cars.

You would have to use the term "Spartan" for the interior of these cars. There were no rear seats, but the factory front bucket seats were retained. The instrument panel was a fiberglass sheet with a block-off plate for the heater location. Interestingly, the only color that could be acquired for the interior was Ford Rangoon Red. The lightweight aspect of the machine was aided greatly by the Plexiglass side and rear windows.

The pair of twin snouts on the front of the fiberglass hood served an excellent purpose in feeding a direct flow of high-speed outside air into the engine.

One of the most-famous factory 1965 A/FX Comets was the former Arnie Beswick car. It has been located and restored. Beswick only drove the car for a short time in 1965 before returning to the Pontiac brand with which he had earlier been associated.

The car then went through a number of different drivers with some changes instituted to it along the way. The car was located and restored by Dave Kunz. The Comet now bears the color and body markings of the original Beswick configuration.

This car was one of the two that carried the fuel injected 427, along with a four-speed top-loader four-speed transmission, and a nine-inch 31-spline locker rear end. This car was only one of two to carry the high-riser engine, the other four came with the SOHC 427.

"The Wedge King" A/FX of Eddy Schartman was another of the highly-recognizable A/FX cars. The car was painted a cold black with white 647 numbers on each side. The car/driver combination brought home the Mr. Stock Eliminator title in the 1965 Winter Nationals.

"Comet Wails" was a 1965 Lincoln-Mercury ad that featured the Hayden Proffitt and Doug Nash Comets.

Another '65 Comet A/FX car was the model driven by Jack Chrisman. The interesting situation was this Comet didn't start out as a 1965 model, but the one-year-earlier model that was earlier discussed. During the 1964 season, the initial Comet was unbeatable, with a blown 427 power plant on nitro with a direct drive power train.

But for the 1965 season, an SOHC engine was installed. The fact that it was a Ford engine made it eligible for Mercury dragsters, and Chrisman and the Sachs & Sons dragster just had to have one.

The '64 Comet was taken to the Stroppe shop for a complete makeover including the installation of a blown SOHC engine. Working in conjunction with Gene Mooneyham, a new blown SOHC engine was constructed. Then the engine was installed with a 25 percent setback on the chassis.

Initially, the "new" car didn't run any faster

Left: *This stock-appearing 1965 B/FX car was the last of this model produced by Bill Stroppe.*

Bottom Left: *The 1965 Comet B/FX interiors had racing-style bucket seats, a floor-mounted shifter, and a plain dashboard. Modern additions here include gauges, a sturdy roll bar and fire extinguisher.*

Bottom Right: *The power plant for this B/FX car is the 289 small block but with a four two-barrel Weber carburetor set-up.*

Jack Chrisman is ready to race his 1965 Comet Cyclone.

Bob Plumer

than the 1964 configuration. But with considerable tuning, the car was able to drop into the nine-second category—9.47 seconds at 165 miles per hour to be exact.

Thankfully, the car has been retrieved and restored by Ford drag car collector Rick Kirk from Ripley, Oklahoma. The car was located in Alberta, Canada, in complete but "…in a very sorry condition. Fortunately, it was surprisingly complete. I made the deal on the car and brought it home," Kirk explained.

The car required a complete ground-up restoration. Rick was also able to locate a correct blown SOHC engine, repair it, and install it in the restoration. One big problem faced in the restoration was locating a direct drive unit.

To that end, Kirk called Chrisman and asked him if he could sketch how the unit looked so that he could possibly reproduce one. Chrisman said he would do much better than that as he still had the original unit in his garage. Rick purchased the unit and was able to complete the restoration to a great degree of accuracy.

Another of the 1965 A/FX cars was found in a most extraordinary manner. John Gotshall of Ohio had long been interested in the A/FX Comet cars and had viewed them when they were racing in the 1960s.

He ended up buying an A/FX after it had been an exhibition racer. Much to his surprise, he found out that it was Hayden Proffitt's former car. Of course, it was far from the way it was when Proffitt had the

car, but Gotshall wanted it to be totally accurate and spent six years getting it to the pristine condition you see here.

The frame of this car had been drilled with many holes for a lightening purpose. Gotshall found out the car was run without the passenger seat and the rear and side windows. The car was also only one of the two original '65 A/FXs that had an altered wheelbase.

Then, there were also the '65 B/FX Comets of which Mercury reportedly constructed two groups of 10 small-block-powered Comet lightweights. Other reports say it was only 15. The power plant of choice was the 289 Hi-Po engine that could produce times in the low 11s in the 120+ miles per hour. With tuning, the 271 stock horsepower could be brought up to 450. And since these cars only weighed in at 2,600 pounds in race trim, the resulting performance was understandable.

An excellent example of a Mercury 1965 B/FX Comet also is owned by Rick Kirk. He explained the Comet had only 106 miles on the odometer, put on a quarter mile at a time.

Kirk explained about his B/FX, "This was probably the last of these cars produced by Stroppe." The originality of the restoration is amazing. First, the trunk and interior are perfect. Then, there are those *original* tires that came with the car. How many factory racer enthusiasts can make that statement about their machine?

It also carries its original Weber carb setup that was available on the 289 engine. The highly-modified engine is capable of some 420 horsepower. Other driveline goodies include a Ford T&C transmission and a Detroit Locker rear end.

Kirk explained that he wanted the restoration to be completely correct. "I even went out and talked to Bill Stroppe about the car."

The car's racing career was a short one according to Kirk, only one year to be exact. "The car was initially purchased from Mercury by Russell and Ronald Dessley who raced the car for the single season. Then, can you believe that it sat outside for a number of years before I made the purchase in 1978. About all I did to it was paint it in the correct Rangoon Red color and freshen up the engine a bit.".

Even with all the Lightweight Ford collectables he owns, this particular B/FX remains one of his favorites. "The factories will never again be involved in manufacturing machines like these. I'm just trying to re-create the nostalgia of those gone-forever days."

Another interesting 1965 Comet B/FX is owned by Bob Schmuki of Waukesha, Wisconsin. He determined that the car was originally campaigned by Bobby Swan for Gateway Ford in Orange, Texas.

Following the 1965 season, the car continued racing and went through a number of different owners. Schmuki was able to locate the car in the upper Midwest, and it was in amazingly excellent condition. It was still carrying period-type Atlas front tires and rear M&H 8.20x15 rears.

The engine used an 8V induction system on the 289 engine, with a pair of 351 Windsor heads and 11-1 forged pistons. The interior of the car carries an original interior, along with a sturdy roll cage and two lightweight seats up front.

1966 Comet Lightweights

Recall that the 1964 and '65 A/FX/B/FX Comets evolved after initially being production line cars before moving to the Bill Stroppe operation for the lightweight/drag race modifications. That extensive company connection decreased in the 1966 drag race program as there were no Ford production line cars built.

These new Comet Lightweights were built from scratch by the Michigan-based Logghe Stamping Company. What evolved was the grandfather of the modern Funny Car. The name of the game for the 1966 turned away from carburetors and went to fuel injection and superchargers.

Mercury, though, was still paying the bills for new lightweight Comets, now sporting a flip-top

Above: *The "Dyno Don" Nicholson funny car in opened position.*
Phil Hall Collection

Left: *A Crane Cam ad from 1966 shows "Dyno Don" Nicholson with his Comet, the car that defined the term "funny car."* Phil Hall Collection

1966 Comet Eliminator I	
Specificaions	
Engine:	Ford/Mercury 427 SOHC V-8, Hilborn fuel injected
Horsepower:	900 hp (estimated)
Body:	Fiberglass replica of Comet shell, Plastigage Corp.
Frame:	Logghe-built chromalloy tubes
Transmissions:	Ford T-10 four speed, Hurst shifter (Two-speed Ford racing automatic available)
Differential:	Detroit Automotive locking with 4.11 ratio
Brakes:	Kelsey-Hayes vented disc
Weight:	1,683 lbs.
Top Speed:	175 mph (estimated)

Source: April 1966 *Hot Rod* magazine

fiberglass body design. Only four of the cars were produced, going to Jack Chrisman, Ed Schartman, the team of Kenz & Leslie, and Don Nicholson.

Mercury engaged Plastigage Corporation to build the first fiberglass body and it was installed on Nicholson's car for the first race of the 1966 season. When the car reached the halfway point of the first race on the track, its body was ripped from the car and thrown high in the air.

But in the long run that season, the fiberglass body would prove to be a real winner for the Mercury team. .

The goal was to keep the cars as stock-appearing as possible, but there was pressure to ease up on that directive.

Nicholson and Schartman kept their cars as stock looking as possible, but that sure wasn't the case with Jack Chrisman. His creation was totally radical with the look of a sleek roadster more than the Comet coupe body from which it was derived.

The top was sawed off of that car and the driver sat deep within the body. Of course, right off the bat the car was considerably lighter than the standard Comet coupe. It ran like a scared rabbit, blazing to speeds of over 180 miles per hour. But that speed would be the reason for the demise of the topless Comet. A parachute failure on the car caused it to overrun the end of the track and crash into a grove of trees.

Chrisman survived the fiery crash, but that would be the end of the unique machine. Mercury officials reportedly told the fireman to let it burn and that was the end of that story.

Mercury management, though, realized that it had made a mistake with the roadster design because it did not look like a factory Comet. The lightweight Comets had been a great merchandising tool for the Lincoln-Mercury Division, and this configuration certainly didn't have that recognition.

The Mercury Factory Team in 1966 had all the answers in match racing competition. The amazing total showed an 85+ percent winning percentage. Nicholson, in his "Eliminator I" Comet, alone had one streak of 30 wins in a row, and overall, just losing 10 times out of 140 races. Doesn't get much better than that!

Much of that success came from his SOHC-injected power plant and the fact that his machine weighed in at a super-lean 1,750 pounds. It was a bad day indeed when 'Dyno Don' ran over 8.2 seconds!

1967 Comet Lightweights

In 1967, Chrisman took delivery of a new Logghe ultra-light 1,620-pound Comet coupe, still with a body resembling a 1967 Comet. With a super-potent SOHC under the hood, the GT-1 got down the track at 191 miles per hour and only used 7.67 seconds to get the job done.

The SOHC power plant in this application was supercharged by a 6-71 blower pushing nitro and that helped push the power figures to a mind-numbing 1,800 horsepower at about 7,800 rpm. A Schiefer magneto was used to fire the Autolite nitro burning spark plugs. With that type of power augmentation, the car was used strictly for match racing.

Also of interest in the car were the changes that were made to counteract the huge torque of the SOHC power plant. Instead of the normal motor mounts, there were extremely rigid front motor plates to contain the explosion of power. .

Incidentally, car magazines at the time described the SOHC as a Mercury engine, but it of course was the engine that was also carrying the Ford name in Ford Lightweights.

The GT-1 transmission consisted of a Ford C6 automatic hooked to a nine-inch narrowed Mercury rear end. It was hoped that there could have been

The Jack Chrisman GT-1 Comet Cyclone is seen in racing action.

Bob Plumer

a wider rear tire stance, but the dimensions of the body dictated that dimension.

The car also used an early coil-over shock front-end suspension system. Also, when the car was completed, 60 percent of the weight rested on the rear wheels, pretty amazing considering the size and weight of the SOHC power plant.

With the one-piece fiberglass body removed, the car had the look of a full-race drag machine. The frame incorporated a full sturdy roll cage with the fuel tank mounted on the front of the frame. On top of the integral roll cage, a special escape hatch was built which allowed Chrisman to exit through the top of the cockpit. To facilitate that action, the hatch was loosely bolted in place.

That frame during that time period was considered to be an example of a high level of fabrication and craftsmanship.

Compared to the frame on that previous year's destroyed car, the location of the engine and driver demonstrated significantly greater engine-and-driver set back. Also, the SOHC engine's huge oil pan reached far below the lower frame rails.

Fortunately, this car is still with us in part, restored and re-created by Jim Barillaro, a longtime lover of the history of these lightweight drag cars. That very same body still sits on an identical-to-the-original type Logghe frame.

He explained the amazing circumstances, "Somehow, the original body had been dumped in a

field and was ready to be crushed. It was happily for me spotted by a guy who just happened to be driving by and he saved it from destruction."

"In 1987, the guy called and told me that the body had Jack Chrisman's name on it! When I checked it out, I confirmed that it was, indeed, the GT-1 Comet." With little hesitation, Jim decided a complete re-creation was warranted.

"I immediately went to work stripping the body. Then I had to find a Logghe chassis to complete the restoration. I finally found a '67 version in New Hampshire and was able to complete the restoration with mostly original-style parts and pieces," Barillaro concluded. "It weighs about 2,300 pounds."

An SOHC 427 mill that closely approximates the original sits proudly in position. The powerhouse swings Venolia 7-1 pistons and has a stock forged Ford crank. A Crane 612A Cam—exactly like Chrisman's—commands the valves. Topside, there's an original-style Mooningham 6-71 blower to push the power figures to a mind-numbing figure.

Jim explained that the original GT-1 drive train would not be duplicated.

"For safety's sake, since I intended to race the car, I decided to use a more modern Lenco two-speed transmission and a Crower clutch."

It should be noted that those modernized pieces don't distract at all from the nostalgic aura the machine emits.

COUGAR AND COMET FOLLOWED
Mercury Racing Successes

In the mid 1960s, Mercury's Comet came onto the drag racing scene. In a few short years, the Mercury Cougar joined the action. Those who knew motor sports recognized the Mercury racing tradition.

The "Big M" had a solid presence in the formative years of NASCAR in the late 1940s. Mercury gained fame as the pride of customizers (the Hirohata and "Rebel Without a Cause" versions). Mercurys also raced in the Carrera Panamericana of Mexico.

Through the decade, their V-8s grew. In 1954, a 256-cid overhead valve V-8 began to get attention. It grew to 292-cid in 1955 and 312-cid in 1956 and '57. By 1964, a healthy 427-cid V-8 was available in 410 and 425-hp versions.

The big Mercurys appealed to road racers, hill climbers, NASCAR Grand National racers and others.

NASCAR embraced Mercurys beginning with Marvin Burke who took Mercury's first Grand National

The popular 1950 Mercurys were favored for rodding, customizing and racing.

win in 1951 on the .625-mile dirt track at the Oakland Stadium just months after Mercury won the 14th race ever sponsored by NASCAR, at Vernon, New York, in 1950.

In 1956, Mercurys won seven major races including Daytona Beach, Florida; Elkhart Lake and Milwaukee, Wisconsin and Phoenix, Arizona. On Aug. 12, 1956, early NASCAR legend Tim Flock drove a Mercury to victory in his final race.

The memorable open-top Mercury convertibles, with their large roll cages and long decks, finished first and third at Daytona Beach. Sam Hanks' Mercury averaged 88.366 mph as he won the 300-mile Trenton, New Jersey, International Speedway race in 1957. Mercurys also finished first at Pomona, California (for the second year in a row) and at Vallejo, California.

Thanks to the prowess of Bill "The Boss" Stroppe, Mercurys became a steady presence in NASCAR racing as well as the Bonneville, Utah, speed trials. Stroppe's efforts were often compared with the work Holman and Moody did for Ford's racing program.

Stroppe and Son Inc. still is involved in Lincoln and Mercury projects.

According to *Automobile Quarterly* in 1987, Stroppe and his team built their famed "Thumper" Mercury as a competitor to the Chrysler 300. The two cars ran at in 1956 at Daytona Beach.

"When [the Thumper] went flying down the beach, it sounded like an airplane," Stroppe recalled.

"We averaged 152 mph…"

A 1964 Mercury stock car with key drivers Joe Weatherly and Parnelli Jones inset.
Phil Hall Collection

The Bill Stroppe-prepared 1957 Mercury Indianapolis 500 Pace Car convertible.

Indianapolis Motor Speedway

Also in 1957, Stroppe prepared the Mercury convertible Indianapolis 500 Pace Car. And he completed his trifecta by preparing 100 special edition Mercurys for the California Highway Patrol.

Stroppe also was responsible for the legendary "Mermaid," a 1957 Mercury convertible outfitted with a hydroplane-style windshield, a combination headrest and long tailfin, bullet-shaped headlight covers and a large X on each door.

In a July 1957 profile, *Hot Rod* magazine noted the Mermaid got its power from a bored '57 Lincoln V-8. The car produced 400+ hp and reached 159.91 mph at the 1957 Daytona Beach Speed Trials.

Hot Rod also showed photos of the Stroppe operation. The racing engine area was as clean and well lighted as a surgery suite. The race chassis prep area also was displayed.

When Pontiac, which dominated NASCAR racing into the early 1960s, had to give up factory-sponsored racing after the 1962 season, Mercury ratcheted up its presence.

Pontiac owner-promoter Bud Moore switched his allegiance from Pontiac to Mercury after the GM ban and brought with him veteran driver Joe Weatherly. The Moore-Weatherly combination became a winning NASCAR presence for Mercury in 1963.

Stroppe performed his work on the 1964 Mercurys, including one driven by Parnelli Jones. The Mercurys dominated NASCAR that season, winning eight straight events. Mercurys also captured the USAC Championship. Mercury drivers Dariel Dieringer and Earl Balmer finished second and fourth at the 1964 Daytona Beach NASCAR race.

The 1964 Mercury also had a strong presence in the famed Pike's Peak Hill Climb.

Mercury had a well-established racing presence just as the economy-minded Comet was making its transformation in NHRA competition. Just three years later, the Cougar was born, a natural in both Trans Am racing and NHRA drag racing competitions.

Today, Mercury has gradually left racing programs to return to its status as luxury car. But there was a time when Mercury left all competitors in the dust.

The 1957 Mercury Monterey stock car was driven to victories by Sam Hanks.
Phil Hall Collection

Another effort at correctness occurred when Jim asked M&H to produce a set of 1967-style 13.00x16 slicks. "M&H used the original molds to make them for me," he revealed.

Watching that scarlet beauty pour on the coal and blast down those 1,320 feet brings back those days almost four decades ago. It's hard to believe that level of lightweight technology that existed during that period.

Barillaro explained the car was also competed in 1968. "It had an updated Logghe chassis, but it was involved in a crash in competition and was later rebuilt.".

Don Nicholson owned a similar machine that was called the "Eliminator II" which was capable of running in the high sevens. The car also sported the flip-top body design and reportedly weighed just over 1,800 pounds.

Late 1960s Lightweights

In 1969, Mercury introduced a new version of its Cougar pony car. It was called the Eliminator. Guess that it's not hard to figure where that name came from as Don Nicholson had been giving Mercury lots of publicity with his fantastic performances through the decade with his "Eliminator" Comets.

Not only did Mercury give the car that name, but also "Dyno Don" Nicholson's name was associated with the car as the driver of one of two drag versions of the model. The other chauffeur was a familiar Mercury driver, Eddie Schartman.

If any American car was bred for racing, it had to be the Cougar. Mercury designers chose to follow the legacy of the race-bred European cars, in part, as they planned the Cougar.

"…we felt [the car] should have more of a European look and image," said Mercury chief designer Buz Griesinger in a retrospective interview in *Automobile Quarterly*. "We wanted a car like the Jaguar…curvaceous and feline in shape and form…"

The "Cat" premiered in the 1967 model year and promptly went racing, especially on the Trans Am circuit as the Dan Gurney Team with cars prepared by Bud Moore. The Moore-prepared Cougars produced 434 hp from the Ford 302 V-8 when prepped with a Crane camshaft, solid valve lifters, roller rocker arms and dual Holley 600-cfm four-barrel carbs. The cars also used Hooker headers and a nine-inch Detroit Locker rear end. With all the additions, the weight was just 2,753 lbs.

In 1968, Cougars also raced in NASCAR's Grand Touring Class and won nine races with Tiny Lund earning the driver's championship. Lloyd Ruby and David Pearson added two wins for the Cat on that circuit.

It was only natural that Cougars would also race on the strip. In September 1968, *Hot Rod* featured the Cougar Eliminator and reported a 7.48-second run at 185.86 mph at the Milan, Michigan drag strip.

The Eliminator street version was initially introduced as a one-of-a-kind concept car to the car show crowd and automotive media to capture pre-production publicity and consumer response.

When the Eliminator was introduced in the 1969 model year, the Boss 302 engine was made available. While the top-gun Boss 429 was on some Eliminator option lists, the engine is only known to have been installed on the two drag versions.

In 1967, Mercury offered a low-production Comet with a 427 engine. The Comet 202 evolved from the factory lightweight experience.

In 1967, this advanced Jack Chrisman GT-1 Mercury Cyclone hit the national scene. It was capable of over 191 mph in the quarter mile.

Above: *Big power came from this SOHC engine, equipped with a 6.71 supercharger. It was capable of producing1800+ horsepower.*

The "little kitty" produced an estimated 1,000 hp with its 6-71 GMC blower, Hilborn fuel injectors and nitro fuel gulped from twin front-mounted tanks. The "Eliminator" used the Logghe chassis with a flip-top Cougar body in fiberglass.

Later in 1968, the "Keaton's Cougar," driven by Dee Keaton of Long Beach, California, was profiled. A former Comet driver, Keaton's "Cat" used a 427-cid Ford SOHC V-8 with a GMC 6-71 blower and the Logghe-bodied setup.

The 1969 Cougars with the Ram Air "Super" Cobra Jet 428 engine were rumored to produce 400 hp in stock form. In drag-prepped versions, the engine made it a fast cat with a 14-second, 104 mph quarter mile recorded during the year.

Whether it was Trans Am S-curves, the NASCAR oval or the straight line drag strips, Mercury's Cougars were as fast, quick and impressive as their namesake. Wherever they raced, they ran to victory.

Street Mercury Lightweights

Although never intended to be drag strip lightweights, during that period, Mercury produced a pair of lightweight/big horsepower street vehicles.

One was a limited production Comet 202 which was built only during the 1967 model year. The company certainly kept with its drag race deployment of the lightweight Comet, and equipped it with a 427/425 horse big block. If there was ever a model built from scratch for the strip, this was it.

Another similar performance model was the Cougar GT-E XR-7. It was a popular street muscle car, but it was also perfect to run in the E Pure Stock drag class. The GT-E, built only in 1968, was 427-powered, was relatively light, and seemed to be set up in the factory for drag racing. The power train contained a C-6 Automatic transmission and a 4.30-geared locker rear end.

One former GT-E owner indicated that he basically took the car from the showroom to the drag strip.

He explained, "The car consistently ran in the 13.70s at about 103 miles per hour on street tires. It never needed traction bars because it really came out hard. It used to clean the muscle cars of the era, including Chevelle, GTOs and big block Trans Ams. I had a ball, that's for sure!"

1968 Cougar Eliminator Funny Car Specificaions	
Engine:	Ford/ Mercury SOHC 427, Hilborn fuel injection and GMC 6-71 blower
Horsepower:	1,000 hp (estimated)
Body:	Fiberglass replica of '68 Cougar, altered
Chassis:	Logghe tubular
Brakes:	Twin Simpson parachutes
Notes:	Water and fuel tanks front mounted for weight distribution. Car has "nose down" design to prevent becoming airborne at speed.
Time/Speed	7.48 seconds at 185.86 mph

Source: Sept. 1968 *Hot Rod* magazine

Chapter 6

PLYMOUTH
LIGHTWEIGHTS

It was a battle royal starting in the late 1961 time period. All the manufacturers took off their gloves and gave it their best shot. They all had potent power plants to offer the public and to dual with on the tracks, and for Chrysler, it was the 413 Wedge engine.

Under the Chrysler banner, both Plymouth and Dodge used much of the same equipment in the engine and transmission departments. (For more on the Dodge Lightweight program, be sure to look at Chapter 3.)

During the 1960s, Plymouth benefited from the Lightweight phenomenon, but didn't have to do anything to acquire that advantage. The frugal, family-oriented tradition of the brand brought ready-made platforms with the nominally-equipped Savoy, Belvedere, Satellite, and Fury models. While Plymouth had been growing in size in 1960 and '61, Chrysler Corporation scaled them down for 1962. By their very nature, they were the lightest mid-sized vehicles—lighter than the Ford and Chevy competition. Much of that lightness was acquired from the Plymouth's unitized body construction.

Starting from that lightweight perspective, then adding different versions of the potent 413 and 426 Wedge engines immediately created some potent 1,320-foot haulers. Here's the story of how it all worked out.

Veteran driver Tom "Mongoose" McEwen drove several Plymouths including this Duster.

Bob Plumer

The "Teacher's Pet" was a 1963 Belvedere Super Stock that raced in the A/SA Class with 426 Wedge power.

1962 Plymouth Lightweights

It was a dark time for the Chrysler Division in early 1962. The sales reports were bleak and the old family image models just weren't getting it done anymore for Plymouth. The burst of enthusiasm for Plymouths that came with the Forward Look era of the 1950s had passed. The market was changing rapidly. Performance was the name of the game, and cars like Pontiac, Ford and Chevrolet were grabbing the headlines. For Plymouth, the fact that the wheelbases were reduced to 116 inches and the new cars lost almost 100 pounds was a step in the right direction.

Things really hit the bulls-eye for Plymouth when they equipped their cars with new lightweight aluminum TorqueFlite three-speed automatics. Plymouth had very much a stock street look with the exception of the lettering on the sides. Many times they dropped a little weight by running without their

hubcaps. It was a look that many performance types liked, and something that started a memorable trend that continues today.

The 1962 413 Stage I Wedge engine used in the Plymouths put out an impressive 410 horsepower. There was even weight-saving accomplished in this

A rear-angle view of the "Honkin' Hemi" car.

This lightweight replica is a 1963 Max Wedge Plymouth that re-creates the former "TAT'R WEDGE" machine.

The predecessor to the 426 Hemi was this 426-Stage III Wedge engine.

engine by use of a one-piece aluminum cross-ram intake topped by a pair of Carter AFB 650-cfm carburetors. For the time period, the engine's 11-1 compression ratio was amazing. An August 1962 *Motor Trend* article described the power plant as the "Plymouth-Dodge Super Stock Engine." The coupling of the engine and tough TorqueFlite automatic continued to enhance the performance image.

On the strip, the Plymouth was an awesome performer in the quarter running in the mid-14 seconds at about 101 miles per hour. Considering that the models were in the 3,000-pound category, that was awesome performance. Everyone in drag racing realized that if the weight could be lightened just a bit, those numbers could come down and up, respectively. That was just around the corner.

A colorful Plymouth Road Runner prepares for its trip down the quarter mile.

With proper tweaking by the Plymouth race teams, the performance would be greatly increased. That performance engine tweaking brought the output to nearly 500 horses in race trim. Tom Grove, in the first of his several "Melrose Missile" Plymouth drag cars, soon demonstrated high-11 second performance at over 118 miles per hour.

There was also a very interesting sidebar story that particular model year. There was a famous name involved, the Granatelli brothers, who made amazing use of a modified and lightened 1962 Golden Commando 413 Max Wedge-powered Plymouth Fury.

First of all, they tested the minimal-weight model the way it came off the showroom floor. It showed an impressive 117.41 miles per hour in 12.51 seconds. They wondered what it would do if the Wedge was punched out to a higher displacement with a pair of Paxton Superchargers in place.

The power boost gave an output of 480 cubic inches. They also added an Isky roller cam and a set of modified Jardine headers. No telling what the horsepower number actually was, but it was certainly out-of-sight!

The Granatellis had hoped to reach the 200-mile per hour figure on the Daytona Beach course. They already held the 184-mph record that they set in 1961. But they had hopes that this machine would run 16 miles per hour faster. The car came very close, but came up just 6 mph short.

But just think about a low-priced, stock passenger Plymouth that was capable of staying on the ground at that speed. It was a totally-awesome accomplishment! It was a new era for performance cars too.

1963 Plymouth Lightweights

There was a change in the engine system with the 1963 model year. The introduction of the 426 Max Wedge engine, basically a slight overbore of the previous 413 V-8, plus the addition of a Racer Brown cam and cast-iron factory headers, created a true performer.

There were actually three versions of the new engine. The smallest version with a single carburetor, was built strictly for stock car racing and had a 400 horsepower capability. The second, the 426 Max Wedge II, mounted a pair of four-barrel carbs on a cross-ram intake manifold and provided 415 horsepower with an impressive 470 lbs.-ft. of torque.

The third version added another 10 horsepower with a 13.5-1 compression ratio, the same cross-ram arrangement, and pounded down 480 lbs.-ft. of torque. Available with these engines was the Plymouth 'Race Package' that contained the 426 Max Wedge engine plus a 727 TorqueFlite transmission, a 4.56 rear end, and a trunk-mounted battery.

Things got interesting when Plymouth offered an aluminum front end and a hood that included a fresh-air hood scoop. In addition to the heater and

Above: *Arlen Vanke's 1963 Plymouth lightweight at a modern drag strip.*

Left: *A second view of the Arlen Vanke Plymouth lightweight.*

This Super Stock clone, an accurate representation of a '64 Belvedere 426 Wedge Super Stock, is owned by Ohio's Mike Pierce.

radio delete, there was also a special factory Super Stock suspension system. Putting the power to the ground was often done with 15-inch racing rubber wrapped around Plymouth's Torq-Thrust lightweight aluminum racing wheels.

Other aluminum parts included the hood, front bumper splash pan, front fenders and bumper brackets. The estimate on all the substitutions was they reduced the vehicle weight by about 150 pounds.

The alterations were such that these cars were initially considered for inclusion into the Factory Experimental Class, but later would be allowed into Super Stock.

The "Golden Commando" was a successful 1963 Plymouth Savoy Super Sport that was campaigned in the Detroit area. The machine

was classified as an SS/SA vehicle. The "Melrose Missile III" was a 1963 Savoy Super Stock car that was driven by Tom Grove. The "Melrose Missile" reached the high 11-second category near season's end and was the 1962 Winternationals Super Stock Champion.

The car earned 26 track records and that performance was fodder for national advertising, and that's exactly what Plymouth did!

When the "Melrose Missile" Savoy was purchased, it carried a steel front end. The aluminum pieces were not available at the time. By mid-year, the aluminum pieces were available and were installed. The car also was equipped with a super-thin front bumper. The inner fenders were removed and that allowed the use of fender well headers—another weight saving step.

Tom Grove's "Melrose Missle" in competition.

Bob Plumer

In addition, the "Melrose Missile III" also sported an aluminum belly pan, bumper brackets, and the radiator crossover. Another interesting bit of 1960s trickery was the car's K-member was shimmed up and rested away from the body. In effect, that lowered the engine and made the front end stand taller.

The "Missile" was recovered and restored by Bob Mosher, owner of Mosher's Muscle Car Motors, which is located in Sun Valley, California. It passed through a number of owners before he made the purchase, just before the cost of these cars vaulted into high rent territory in some cases. Bet the previous owners today are sorry now that they ever let it go!

In 2002, a low mileage, 1963 Savoy Max Wedge from California, complete with a four-on-the floor, sold at auction for $54,000. If you have the cash, they still can be found!

Through the years, there were a number of Melrose Missiles built—about a half-dozen to be exact—but Mosher will tell you that this one was the most successful.

1964 Plymouth Lightweights

The Super Stock wars were going strong in this model year, and Plymouth was one of the big players. The Super Stock Plymouths, which were still exclusively using the Savoy body style, were basically race cars that could be used on the street. Engineers combed the guts out of these cars to find anyplace that could be stripped and lightened.

Besides the expected heater and radio delete, there was also no rear seat (definitely not the car if you had a family), both sun visors (not good for a sunny day situation), and it was a little hard on the ears as all the sound deadener was omitted. You could acquire a special package tray to cover where the missing back seat should have been.

Your shoes rested on ultra-thin carpeting, and the austere, nonadjustable A-100 Dodge van seats left something to be desired as far as comfort was concerned.

On certain pieces, there was a choice of either aluminum or acid-dipped sheet metal. In most cases, it was aluminum that was used. Portions of the car made from aluminum were the hood, including the functional hood scoop, and the front end, including the fenders. Like earlier models, stock Plymouth metal was removed on the low-rear portion of the front fenders to accommodate the aftermarket fender well-exit headers.

The 1964 model year marked the final year of the Max Wedge engine, the final Stage III version in this case. It was basically replaced later in the season with the iron-headed 426 Hemi that carried the same 425-horse factory rating at a 13-1 compression ratio.

One point worth making about these cars was that even though the diameters of the rear tires were growing, there was no tubbing done to accommodate them. Instead, there was a narrowed rear end that accomplished the same effect.

The front bumper was NOT one you'd like to have in an accident because it was so razor-thin. The standard for all the lightweights was to install the battery (with vent hoses) over the right-rear tire and that aided in

This 1964 Plymouth Super Stock clone looks real with the period-type wheels, tires and hood scoop.

Phil Hall Collection

weight transfer. The spare tire was mounted on that same side in the trunk.

A rare metal, also light, found its way into these '64s in the form of factory lightweight magnesium front wheels. Also, only the driver had a windshield wiper.

Interestingly, these Plymouths did not have roll bars installed when they were delivered. That was the responsibility of the crew. What crews also considered their responsibility was to further lighten the cars from their 3,200-pound delivery weight. It was reported that as much as 300 more pounds of weight could be eliminated. One common deletion was the high beam headlights.

National Street Car Association(NSCA) President Tony DePillo has a great example of a '64 Super Stock

Savoy painted in the red and white colors with striped roof of the famous "Honkin' Hemi" machine. The car was a significant performer setting a National B Super Stock Record of 9.09 seconds at 147 miles per hour.

Tony has had the car for a dozen years. "It's an excellent example of a period Super Stock Car which is getting very hard to find these days," he explained. "The car carries a 426 Hemi power plant and it's an unbelievable performer. I would have to describe it as a violent car. I leave the line between 7,200 to 7,800 rpms and it shifts at about 8,100."

The Hemi on the DePillo Savoy is the Drag Hemi equipped with an aluminum cross-ram intake and 770-cfm of induction. The factory was still saying it was equal to 425 horses, but everybody knew that

The famous "Mr. 5 and 50" name was carried on a number of SS cars during the 1960s. This is the 1964 Plymouth version.

Jack Biel

was a joke, being probably well over the 500 figure in reality.

The so-called "Super Commando" 426 Hemi was officially released in February 1964 and was a heavy player in Super Stock racing starting then and lasting a number of years with improved versions. There were a large number of Hemi engines built that model year, going into both Plymouth and Dodge models. For the Plymouths of that model year, it took an extra two grand to get one resting under your hood.

The Hemi sported a forged crank, impact extruded pistons, cross-bolted main bearing caps, forged rods, solid lifters, a header-style exhaust system, a 328-degree cam, and stiffer valve springs.

The Hemis could also be bought right over the Plymouth parts counter, but of interest for this subject area, was that they were now coming as standard equipment for the Plymouth Super Stock cars.

If there was ever a totally-recognizable 1964 Plymouth Lightweight, it was the "LAWMAN" of Al Eckstrand. No mistaking the model that had those huge letters on each door. Initially starting out with Max Wedge III power, it reverted to the Hemi when it became available.

"Those were great years," Eckstrand recalled in *Mopar Muscle* magazine. "Drag racing was a young sport... It was a wonderful time."

He recalled a match race in Super Stock with his Plymouth versus Dick Landy's Dodge at the York (Pennsylvania) US 30 Dragway, near Pittsburgh.

"That was an amazing event, I'll never forget it. They had so many people that they finally had to let them in for free. It seemed like it was just run after run after run."

1965 Plymouth Lightweights

The Plymouth Super Stock dominance that had started in 1964 would be continued this model year if Chrysler management had anything to say about it. The company would manufacture 160 A990 Belvedere Satellite Hemi Lightweights to do battle at both the national and local level.

The "Race Hemi" engine carried a number of lightweight aluminum components as its contribution to the vehicle lightness. Included were aluminum cylinder heads, oil-pump body, water-pump housing, water-outlet elbow and alternator bracket. Also, the cross-ram intake manifold was fabricated of cast magnesium. It was capable of

This 1965 Super Stock Plymouth clone shows the tremendous interest that remains for these cars.

reaching a reported 600 horsepower from the factory.

In this configuration, the Hemi was connected to the A-833 four-speed tranny. The transmission was lightened with an aluminum housing, and was controlled by a column-mounted stick shift. There were 4.56 gears within an 8 ¾-inch unit.

There were, however, changes in the material rules for the bodies. The major difference was that aluminum front ends were no longer allowed by NHRA. The bodies were forced to use the standard factory thickness. Such, however, was not the case with the hood, hood scoop, doors and fenders that were .020 inches thinner with a .018-inch thickness.

While the rear bumper was stock, there was considerable lightening to the front bumper that was only .040 inch thick with lightweight mounting brackets. It certainly wouldn't have been much protection in a highway crash.

The cars had a very austere external look with painted wheels and no wheel covers. There certainly wasn't much of a variety for inside colors as only champagne red was available.

The seating was accomplished using the gaunt A-100 Dodge van seats. The remainder of the interior was cleaned out! You could forget the creature comforts!

There was the expected heater and radio delete, along with the omission of such items as the rear seat, arm rests, trim panels, dome light, visors, and even the coat racks.

It's not a well-known fact, but the highly publicized Pontiac Super Duty cars were not the only Lightweight to use the Swiss Cheese, multi-holed frames. The technique was used on these cars and the frame material used was aluminum. The suspension system was also lightened with the elimination of the front sway bars and the K-member. The torsion bars were the smaller diameter type used with the six-cylinder engine models. Of course, the smaller diameter also meant lighter weight.

With the weight eliminated using the aluminum front end, it was also necessary to eliminate more weight to achieve the desired weight transfer effect.

One of the most-famous of these 1965 Belvedere Satellites was the "Drag-On-Lady" model driven by Shirley Shahan, who competed in the S/SA Class. She turned a best quarter mile time of 129.30 miles per hour. The July 1990 *Muscle Car Review* described its performance as follows, "It had the gusto to run at the head of the pack, and styling-wise we scored it high too."

Then, there was also Butch Leal in his 1965 "California Flash" Satellite that won the S/S Class at the Indy Nationals. And how can you forget the Belvedere Lightweight of Grumpy Jenkins who wheeled the car to the NHRA S/S World Championship? .

The Plymouth brand scored a rare double in the 1965 Winter Nationals with Bill Andress scoring in Super Stock, while Bill Jenkins came home first in Super Stock Automatic. Jenkins also took the Top Stock Class with an 11.39-second dash. In the 1965 Nationals, Butch Leal won Super Stock.

What was really amazing about the '65 Plymouth lightweight was its longevity. The model continued to win with Leal taking Super Stock and Shirley Shahan winning Top Stock in the '66 Winter Nationals. In

A 1965 altered Plymouth is ready for drag racing competition.

The "El Toro" is a restoration of an original '65 Hemi Super Stocker that was converted to an A/FX configuration in 1966.

the 1966 Spring Nationals, 1965 Plymouths took Super Stock with Ed Miller driving and Super Stock Automatic featuring Joe Smith at the wheel.

In fact, the 1965 Plymouth would continue to consistently win until the introduction of the '68 Barracuda lightweight. The 1965 Plymouths would win both Super Stock and Super Stock Automatic in the 1967 Winter Nationals and Super Stock/B in the 1968 Winter Nationals.

1965 Plymouth A/FX

The big news for 1965 was the introduction of an Altered Wheelbase (AWB) /Factory Experimental drag car design. It was one of the wildest things that had ever been seen on the national drag racing scene at that time. The class would compete under the A/FX and B/FX categories, depending on the size of the engine being used. Even though there were radical changes in these models, there wasn't a significant change in the external looks of the car. Plymouth felt they could be used as an advertising tool.

The body style for the reported six AWB designed Plymouths built, was the rakish Belvedere hardtop body style, also used by the Dodge Coronet. The altered wheelbase process started with a so-called Body-in-White. Surprisingly, the body was manufactured in a different production facility than the Super Stock versions.

The first procedure was unlike anything that had ever occurred before. The body was "acid dipped,"

a bath that in effect removed about 200 pounds of metal weight. The process was definitely a winner in terms of weight reduction, but a loser in the effect the chemicals had on the sheet metal. The metal was corroded and the process caused structural weakening. That's one of the main reasons why so few of these cars remain today.

The next procedure required Plymouth to use an aftermarket manufacturer, Amblewagon Corporation in Troy, Michigan. Normally they were a company that built vehicles such as ambulances.

The process at Amblewagon involved a lateral cut which took 15 inches from the center of the floor pan in front of the rear wheel housings. Then, the two remaining sections were welded back together. Next the rear wheel wells and immediate body area were removed and moved 15 inches forward to correspond with the altered floor surface.

Finally the 15-inch space left by the movement of the wheel wells was filled in with the section removed from in front of the wheel wells. To cover all this cutting and joining, the entire floor pan area was filled and finished.

With a change of that magnitude, it was necessary to bring forward the spring mounting locations for body integrity purposes.

Other changes to bring this "new car" together involved a significant modification of the front end with a new curved front pan and replacement of the K member with rectangular members. The inner

This version of the "Melrose Missile," driven by Tom Grove, is an early example of the famed Plymouth factory altered lightweight drag racers.

fender panels were also modified with the movement of the upper control arm supports 10 inches forward. That effectively moved the front wheels forward the same distance.

Rather than modify the front fenders to house the new location of the wheel cutouts, special lightweight fiberglass pieces from the Plaza Fiberglass Manufacturing Company were used. In addition to the fenders, the front doors, lift-off hood and scoop, front bumper, and rear deck were also made available by Plaza, and many of the teams used those lightweight parts.

There was also a fiberglass dash panel that had no glove box or radio cutouts.

All the fiberglass pieces weighed in at about 80 pounds, which resulted in the saving of about 200 pounds over the sheet metal versions. If you wanted to buy all these fiberglass points, it would lighten your billfold by $410.

The look of the car after this strenuous redo was hard to believe. There was so much length between the rear axle centerline and the end of the car, actually a very short distance behind the back edge of the passenger door. It was an unforgettable look, but one certainly optimized for weight transfer to the rear driving wheels. They looked funny and earned the name "funny cars."

The now 2,800-pound Belvederes had basically the same lightweight interior that was carried by its Super Stock brethren. That included the Dodge van seat, along with the Super Stock door, quarter trim panels and carpeting. Of course, there was also the required roll cage installed. Finally, the Plexiglass side windows and Lexan windshield were lightweight pieces used.

This was a factory-supported building of a full-out drag race machine. It was definitely a measure of

the level of performance competition among the Big Three, and a phenomenon that will most certainly never return again.

A number of the Plymouth Factory Teams received these A/FX cars including Butch Leal and H. L. Shahan ("California Flash"), Ronnie Sox and Buddy Martin ("Paper Tiger Too"), Tom and Charles Grove ("Melrose Missile"), and Lee Smith and Al Eckstrand with the "Golden Commandos."

Buddy Martin recalled troubles negotiating a contract with Mercury for the 1965 season and that things fell into place to race with Plymouth with his teammate Ronnie Sox. They first saw the new altered Plymouth in November 1964.

"…we were very pleasantly surprised when we got our first look at the cars," Martin recalled in a 1995 edition of *Mopar Performance*. "We knew right then that they would be very competitive. Ronnie was very excited about driving our new Plymouth."

All these cars used the Race Hemi power plant, but demonstrated increased performance from the use of Hilborn Fuel Injection, alcohol, nitro methane, and later even supercharging.

Interestingly, the radical factory-built Plymouths were quickly outlawed by NHRA after running in just a few events. The cars, though, continued to be very popular in match races before huge crowds.

Sox and Martin ran their Plymouth in 9.98 seconds in April 1965 at U.S. 30 Drag-O-Way in York, Pennsylvania. Butch Leal ran a solo run in his Plymouth altered "California Flash" at the Winternationals.

What happened with some of the Mopar runners that were not in the elite factory group and didn't get one of the AWB machines? It came down to one thing. You had to build one yourself.

Take the case of dragster Jon Thorne who, at the time, was wheeling a '63 Plymouth lightweight, the "Jayhawker." What he accomplished to run in 1965 competition was come up with a homemade A/FX machine.

It accomplished the same effect as the factory A/FX cars. He moved the rear wheels 15 inches forward and the wheel openings were sectioned and moved up. A Dodge truck straight axle replaced the K-frame. The rear wheels on the Thorne modification were not as far forward as those on the factory AWB cars. A portion of the homemade car also used fiberglass panels.

It went through several owners before it was obsolete against the all-fiberglass creations that came onboard starting in 1966. Later, Chet Gibbs would acquire the remains of the car and accomplished a complete restoration.

1966 Lightweights

As there was not a factory lightweight released for the 1966 season, many of the top Plymouth teams continued using the same equipment from the previous year. That was the case with the "Melrose Missile" and the "California Flash" vehicles.

One of the new machines of interest was the super-light Barracuda of the Sox and Martin team. The 1966 lightweight Plymouth of Jere Stahl was one of the most successful of these cars, taking every A Stock event except for the Winter Nationals. The Coronet 440 and Belvedere I two-door post cars were the models of choice.

Shirley Shahan, in her '65 "Drag-On-Lady" Plymouth, won the NHRA Top Stock Eliminator.

1967 Race Package Cars

"23" was the magic number for Chrysler during 1967 as both Plymouth and Dodge were provided with the so-called "Race Package Cars."

For Plymouth, the designation was RO23J7, where the R stood for B Body, O for the Super Stock Class, and 23 for two-door hardtop. The Hemi was identified by the J, while the 7 indicated the 1967 model year. The 150 cars that were built that year were equally divided between the two Chrysler brands.

Right: *This 1966 ad really flaunts the Plymouth Lightweight drag success by showing the cars of Shirley Shahan, Jere Stahl and others.*

PLYMOUTH PUT FUN IN THE
Lightweight Barracudas

When the Plymouth unveiled the 1964 ½ Barracuda, within days of the Ford Mustang's debut, it was meant as an eye-catching, practical and fun vehicle.

Little did Plymouth know how much fun drag racers would have with the Barracuda. Drivers included Arlen Vanke, Judy Lilly, Ronnie Sox and Buddy Martin and NASCAR legend Richard Petty. A few "fabulous fish" are profiled or pictured here.

The Hurst Hemi Under Glass

The Hurst Hemi Under Glass is probably one of the most memorable versions of the Barracuda.

It even appeared in Chrysler Corporation commercials on the "Bob Hope Show" in 1965.

Hot Rod profiled the car in its April 1965 issue.

"The Hurst gang...selected a '65 Barracuda to be stuffed full of 426 Plymouth Hemi," said the article. "...the idea struck them that it would be much simpler to place the mill in the back and

The famous Hurst Hemi Under Glass Barracuda.

Phil Hall Collection

to begin their work from there."

Steps taken by the Hurst crew included:

—Removing the radiator, 273-cid Commando V-8, transmission, standard rear axle and more.

—Fabricating a square tubing sub-frame to support the engine.

—Flipping a large Mopar differential to accept input from the rear.

—Replacing stock fenders with acid-dipped versions and adding Plexiglass windows.

—Inserting long truck-type heater ducts to get air from the cowl to the Holley carbs.

—Using a pair of industrial blowers to force air over the radiator and exhaust it out the back.

The result was a 2,300-lb. car that became famous in drag racing exhibitions, although not quite according to plan said early driver "Wild Bill" Shrewsberry.

"Originally, Hurst Product Planning designed the car to go fast. The spectators really dug seeing the car, so it became a wheelie car," Shrewsberry told writer John Dianna in 1970.

"...hittin' second gear with the car pointed toward the sky took some strong nerve-buildin' on my part. I've broken a few front axles," he added. "I've turned over three times in five years."

The 1966 version was driven by Bob Riggle and included a Plexiglass panel mounted in the firewall below the dash so Riggle could see the track while guiding the car in wheelie position.

It ran with a 1,500-hp 426 Hemi engine and a 727 TorqueFlite transmission that was coupled with

Tom "Mongoose" McEwen drove this Barracuda for a Plymouth Dealers' association. Bob Plumer

The "King Fish" was a good name for this royal Barracuda drag racer. Bob Plumer

a Casale V-drive to a reversed and flipped rear end so the ring and pinion gears ran forward.

The Hurst Hemi Under Glass made many friends for the slope-backed Plymouth.

The Other Wheel Standing Barracuda

In 1965, there was another famous wheel standing Barracudas, built in California by B and M Hydro of Van Nuys. It had many fiberglass body parts and its backlight was slotted for air flow.

The rear-mounted Hemi engine was designed to run on 80-percent nitro at 1,200 to 1,400 hp with a 6.5:1 compression ratio.

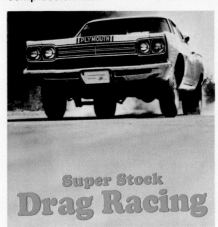

The first version suffered extreme lift at high speeds. Tom "Mongoose" McEwen once pushed the car over 150 mph and it reared up and flipped, destroying everything but the engine. McEwen survived the wreck.

The second version featured redesigned rear suspension that coped with the extreme torque. Pivot points in the sub-chassis raised the rear portion of the car insuring positive pressure over the front wheels. This Barracuda hit 9.06 seconds at 168.54 mph with McEwen behind the wheel.

The Chi-Town Hustler

By 1968, the team of John Farkonas, Austin Coil and Pat Minick of Summit, Illinois, produced a memorable funny car with the unforgettable name, the "Chi-Town Hustler."

Based on a 1968 Barracuda, their creation featured a body by Fiber Glass Ltd., a tube chassis made by the team, Logghe front and rear suspension and a blown Hemi V-8. Later, the team raced a Dodge Charger

This image, from Plymouth factory literature, shows they were serious about drag racing. Phil Hall Collection

The Ed Miller Barracuda is center stage in this period Valvoline ad. Phil Hall Collection

version under the same name.

The car is synonymous for many with famous drag racing ads with the famed drag racing radio tag voiceover screaming "Sunday, Sun-day, SUN-DAYYY."

Other famous Barracuda drag racers included Candies and Hughes, the King Fish, Big John Mazmanian, McEwen's "Mongoose," and Don Schumacher.

1966 Plymouth Hemi Specificaions	
Engine:	426 Hemi V-8
Horsepower:	425 hp
Torque:	490 lbs-ft.@ 5,000 rpm
Transmission:	Hurst four speed
Cylinders:	Cast iron
Clutch:	11-inch Borg and Beck
Tires:	Firestone Super Sports Wide Oval
Notes:	Hooker headers
Weight:	3,904 lbs.
Price:	$3,600
Top Speed:	14.34 seconds @ 102.72 mph (stock) 13.69 seconds @ 105.5 mph (drag tires/tube headers)

Source: May 1966 *Hot Rod* magazine

B Stock was the class originally set for the cars, but because of the way the cars were equipped, NHRA determined that they would be run in Super Stock D class.

The longstanding Belvedere model was again the selected body style because of its lighter weight. The Street Hemi was the standard engine that included extras like a Vanke intake manifold, dual Carter AFB carbs, special deep oil pan, transistor ignition, and a special Prestolite dual-point tach drive. As in earlier times, the factory 425 horsepower rating was totally ridiculous. The power train continued with a factory four-speed transmission that was attached to a Dana 60 rear end.

With lightened weight still being of the highest priority, the model was stripped of just about everything that wasn't welded in position. That included the wheel covers, the expected radio and heater, body insulation, the carpet pad, and body sealers. It goes without saying that the battery was resting in the right-rear corner of the trunk.

Actually, the RO23 program, along with its companion WO Dodge effort, was just a preliminary program to what would come for the 1968 season.

Even so, there were some notable wins for the model when Ronnie Sox took the Super Stock

Eliminator Class at the 1967 Spring Nationals, which he duplicated the next year in the same class at the 1968 Spring Nationals.

1968 Lightweight Barracudas

The Barracuda and the counterpart Dodge Dart, were considered as the ultimate factory lightweight effort, and the results of the model on the drag strip proved it. In fact, over four decades later, some of these cars (along with similar clones) are still out there competing, and winning!

The first of these Barracudas was the so-called factory mule car. It was totally recognizable with the Plymouth name plastered across the doors. The longstanding relationship with Hurst was again evident in the preparation of the cars. An interesting aspect of these unique Barracudas was they were A Body cars instead of the previous B Bodies.

Lightweight work was substantial, to say the least. On the body, fiberglass was the light material of choice with the fenders, hood, and hood scoop fabricated of the material. A new super-thin .080-inch thick material called Chemcor was used in the windows.

For more weight saving, the rear seat was removed and lightweight bucket seats were used. The other lightening was pretty much status quo with previous years. This included radio and heater delete, no outside mirrors or windshield wipers, no right side seat belts, no window cranking mechanicals, and the deletion of the sound deadener and body sealer materials.

Hurst received the Barracudas from Chrysler for the modifications without the engine and transmission, front sheet metal and bumpers and or the side window glass. Little was done externally to differentiate them from their street legal "brothers." In fact, it was left to the customer to paint the car in whatever colors were desired.

Hurst gutted the interior and the appropriate race changes were made. The company also added the Hurst shifter and installed a Super Stock rear axle capable of handling a number of different ratio gears.

The Hemi now sported hemispherical heads, twin Holley 780-cfm carbs, Hooker Headers, deep groove belt pulleys, a seven-blade aluminum fan, and a high-volume oil pump. It was now reportedly capable of 650 horsepower. The cars were capable of 10-second dashes down the strip at 130 miles per hour. The cars were available either automatic or four-speed manual transmissions. The automatic was a 727 TorqueFlite with a manual valve body, stall converter, heavy-duty

Coming this way, the Hurst Hemi Under Glass Barracuda!
Bob Plumer

internals, and the Hurst floor-mounted shifter. The 8-3/4 rear end came with 4.86-1 gearing.

The stick-shift was an A-833 four-speed with the Hurst floor shifter with reverse lock-out. It also contained a 10-1/2-inch clutch/flywheel package and a high-strength steel bell housing.

One of the finest restorations of the breed is the former "Mr. Five and Fifty" Barracuda that was driven by Jack Werst during the 1968, 1969, and 1970 seasons. Then it went to other owners where it was campaigned until 1987.

There's also the "Arlen Vanke Jegs" machine that has been restored to amazing accuracy. In fact, Arlen Vanke put together the engine for owner Lee Hodge. The old Super Stocker carries its original A-833 transmission and 4.56-geared Dana rear end. Vintage Drag 500 racing slicks provide the traction.

Among the many 1968 Barracudas was the flashy machine of female driver Judy Lilly in her "Miss Mighty Mopar" Cuda. She raced the machine in the Super Stock AA Class.

Ronnie Sox was a big winner in one of the '68 Barracudas, winning repeatedly with both the NHRA and AHRA groups. The '68 Barracuda quickly showed that the Hemi-powered car was ready to monopolize the competition. It did such a thing at the 1968 Nationals when he won three of the top four classes.

Included was Willey Cossey taking Super Stock/B, Gary Osrich taking Super Stock/A Automatic, and Alen Vanke taking Super Stock Eliminator. Fred Hurst took his Barracuda to a Street Eliminator win at the World Finals. And all were done while driving 1968 Hemi Barracudas.

In 1969 the trend would continue as Ronnie Sox took the Sox and Martin Barracuda to wins at the Springnationals, Nationals and World Finals, becoming the 1969 World Champion drag racer.

And the teens had a hero as well when 17-year-old high school student Mark Coletti became the '69 Winternationals Stock Eliminator champion in his '68 Barracuda.

Since that year, Barracudas have continued to run strong. In fact, Allyn Lee took his Hemi 'Cuda to a record run of 8.97 seconds in the NHRA SS/A class in 1995. The Plymouth Lightweights set some unforgettable records in the 1960s and beyond. They made some vivid impressions on the strip.

Chapter 7

PONTIAC
LIGHTWEIGHTS

It wasn't Chevy, but the Pontiac Division of General Motors that was the first to build lightweight drag cars. In fact, Pontiac put its foot in the racing door as early as 1957 when it had connections with early NASCAR racers.

In drag racing, the competition initially came from the Chevy Division when it issued its multi-carbed 265/283 Power Packs in the mid-1950s. Pontiac was also involved in performance, and in 1956, came out with a 285 engine with two four-barrel carbs, followed by a potent Tri-Power and fuel-injected 317 engine in 1957. The 370-cid engine soon followed in 1958. In 1960, the first 389 Super Duty heads became available, and the performance beat continued with the 1960 Super Duty Catalina.

1960 Super Duty Catalina

This model sported an awesome 389-cid engine complete with the Super Duty Package and a Tri-Power carb setup capable of 363 horsepower. It was soon learned that 395 ponies was the actual dyno reading.

Arnie Beswick's Tempest in period racing action.

Mention 389 cubes and a Tri-Power induction system, and most Pontiac fans would immediately think GTO. This was four years

Bob Plumer

The colorful "Brutus" Pontiac Tempest drag racer got attention on the drag strip.

Bob Plumer

earlier when the big cars and their 389s were getting their share of attention in drag and oval track racing.

In February 1960, Arnie Beswick took his Tri-Power, four-speed Catalina to victory at the NHRA/NASCAR Winternationals. During the 1960 NHRA Nationals, Pontiac ad agency employee Jim Wangers proved the capabilities of an early Super Duty when he won the Stock Eliminator Class. His 1960 Catalina carried the 389 S/D engine prepared by Royal Pontiac.

Rumors had it that the Wangers car was also modified with some lightweight aluminum front components. Royal Pontiac would later play heavily in the Pontiac lightweight drag success with Wangers at the wheel a majority of the time.

The S/D engine in these cars was modified with high performance equipment such as custom solid lifter camshafts, special carburetion, and internal engine changes.

The great stuff for Pontiac was just getting started, and in the next few years of high-performance lightweight competition it would be the brand to beat much of the time.

Bob Plumer

Harold Ramsey's 1960 "Union Park" Pontiac was a winner early in the decade.

The Royal Pontiac at the 1960 NHRA Nationals at Detroit Dragway.

1961 Pontiac Catalina Super Duty

One of the more successful 1961 Super Dutys was owned and raced by Bob Harrop of Camden, New Jersey. You would have to say that Harrop was in the know as far as Pontiac performance, being a mechanic at Dave Cole Pontiac in Pennsauken, New Jersey.

The car was ordered as a two-door sedan model, with a flat roof rather than the popular "bubble top" then used by Pontiac and Chevrolet, to save considerable weight. Harrop also specified both radio and heater deletes and the soundproofing and factory undercoating were omitted. There was big weight-savings using thin aluminum front and

rear bumpers. Harrop didn't even want the tools that usually came with the car, or even the spare tire!

The solid black Harrop Catalina carried the 389 S/D engine, which carried all the performance features of that powerful mill. Listed at 389 horsepower, it was estimated to actually produce more than 400 horsepower. And in particular, this '61 Super Duty was fitted with a special NASCAR radiator, custom suspension, and even a special severe duty rear axle with a 3.90 posi rear end.

The Harrop Pontiac used a McKellar solid lifter camshaft, plus such SD features as a four-bolt

Jim Wangers ran 102.04 mph in 14.14 seconds with the Royal Super Stocker and cleaned house at the NHRA Nationals.

The famous tri-carb setup in the performance Pontiac's engine bay.

Mike Mueller

main block, SD heads, a forged crankshaft, rods and pistons as well as a high volume oil pump, cast aluminum factory headers, the Pontiac Tri Power intake with mechanical linkage and cut out plates for the exhaust.

Its record was remarkable during that 1961 season where the car was campaigned in some 44 states. Harrop won consistently, which ended up earning him a Hurst sponsorship.

There were big wins at the 1962 Daytona Speed Week where he mowed down all the top drag teams of the period.

At the end of the grueling seven-day event, he had won the title of "Mr. Stock Eliminator" and became the national advertising model for Pontiac's national advertisements.

The old Super Duty went through a number of other owners before it was retired in 1971. During that

You just can't get enough of the pretty—and powerful—1961 Pontiac Super Duty Catalinas.

Mike Mueller

Above: *The famous Pontiac 421-cid Super Duty V-8 restored and resplendent.* Mike Mueller

Right: *Both Hurst and Pontiac promoted the floor-mounted three-speed shifter in 1961.*

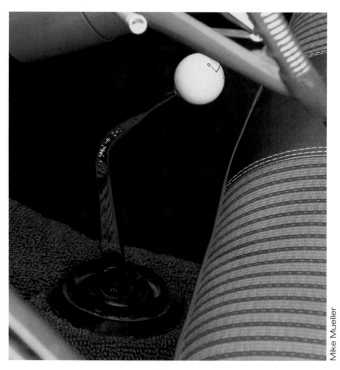

Mike Mueller

Recipe for a Hotter 1961 Pontiac

	Drag Racing Choice	Kit/Part Number
Engine:	Trophy 425-A (348 hp)	# 989761
	w/hd oil pump and pan	# 989644
Crankshaft:	Forged steel	# 533038
Bearings:	Clevite F77	# 531677
	Moraine 400	# 534677
Pistons/rods:	Forged True piston package	# 989643
	Thompson piston package	# 989666
Cylinder heads:	Heavy duty w/ 1.92 intake and 1.660 exhaust valves	# 989798
Camshaft:	McKeller # 7 kit	# 983507
	McKeller # 8 kit	# 983508
Manifolds:	Cast iron kit	# 983503
Ignition:	Heavy duty package	# 989764
Spark plugs:	A22 Autolite, J63-T Champion or AC 42 Commercial	
Exhaust:	Cast iron headers	# 989832
Other:	Pulleys & balancer kit	# 989794
	Clutch fan	# 988938
	Three speed floor mount kit	# 983550
	Aluminum front bumper	# 540804
	Aluminum rear bumper	# 540805

Source: March 1961 *Hot Rod* magazine

period, there was still time to set an NHRA record in its class of 115 miles per hour in 11.8 seconds.

Pontiac superstar Arnie Beswick was also a strong runner during the 1961 season in his "Passionate Poncho." It was practically unbeatable, having never lost a match race or a Super Stock Class race. Beswick was the overall winner at the 1961 NASCAR Winternationals at Daytona Beach, he won the Ultra Stock Class at the World Series, and the NHRA Summer Nationals at Indy.

Beswick explained that his '61 Super Duty was his favorite. He initially ran the car in its stock 348 horsepower version, but found that he needed extra performance. "So I bolted on the Super Duty Package and got the job done."

Hayden Proffitt was successful driving Mickey Thompson's 1961 Super Duty (that was carrying one of the first 421 S/D power plants) and won the Optional Super Stock Class at the 1961 Indy Nationals. Mickey drove a 389 Super Duty at the nationals, but was beaten by Beswick.

Not only was the 389 S/D pounding out victories with NHRA and IHRA, but it was also equally effective with a single carburetor in high-speed NASCAR oval-track competition. At Daytona in February 1960, a 389 Super Duty set a new speed record of 155+ miles per hour with Fireball Roberts at the wheel. Marvin Panch, in a Smokey Yunick-prepared Catalina, won the Daytona 500, with Roberts and Jim Weatherly in Pontiacs taking the two 100-mile preliminary races.

1962 Super Duty Catalinas/Grand Prixs

The competition was coming on quick, so Pontiac decided that it was necessary to make some changes for the next model year. It came from two directions, both under the hood and on the scales.

In the power department, there was a complete turnover to the new 421 Super Duty power plant. The powerhouse was capable of an advertised 405 horses. In reality, it was probably over 500 horsepower. After massaging by race teams, who's to say what the horsepower figure was?

The 421 S/D was actually a stroked version of the 389. Special parts and pieces in this power plant included the likes of a pair of Carter AFB four-barrel carbs on a Pontiac designed and manufactured intake manifold. It perked in conjunction with a super-impressive 11 to 1 compression ratio, but there was also a 12.5 to 1 option that could be obtained over the counter and provide even more power.

The engine used a heavy-duty block with four-bolt steel main caps for the trio of center main bearings. Its racing purpose really came to light with the use of Mickey Thompson forged aluminum pistons on Super Duty forged steel rods driving a Pontiac forged steel crankshaft. Most of the front-line drag teams used a functional ram-air-style hood scoop.

The Pontiac engineers paid considerable attention to the exhaust manifolds that were cast from either steel (which the engines came from) or an optional lightweight aluminum unit that made a small contribution to reducing overall weight.

They worried about those aluminum headers, but due to the short time period of engine operation during drag operation, no problems developed. The headers couldn't be used with NASCAR Super Dutys because of the long engine operation.

An article in the April 1962 *Hot Rod* Magazine described the Super Duty's exhaust manifold as having "...tuned pairing of the passages on each side so that firing impulses are spread with two

large branch outlets in each manifold...They are very efficient with dual outlets on each side joining together in an adaptor flange which then dumps into the exhaust pipes."

A heavy-duty oil pump was used to support the overpowering performance of the power plant. The engine tach usually was mounted by the drag teams in front of the driver on the top of the dashboard.

There was much more, like a high-capacity fuel pump, Moraine aluminum bearings, a deep-sump high-capacity oil pan, and a Pontiac dual-point distributor. The extra performance was coupled with either a close or wide ratio T-10 four-speed or a T-85 Borg Warner three-speed tranny.

NHRA was worried about some of the factory teams using engines that weren't available to the general public. It was eventually decided by the governing body that a certain number of the engines and cars had to be produced before the model was eligible for Super Stock competition.

Pontiac responded by building more than the required number of the 421 S/D engines for public consumption. The engines were offered on the Grand Prix Sport Coupes and Catalinas.

Competition was enhanced by the car's lightweight aspects—like the aluminum front fenders, inner fenders, hood, radiator brackets, and grille. Also, there were aluminum bumpers and a dealer option of a Plexiglass windshield. The aluminum parts were stamped from the same dies used on the steel pieces. The lightweight modifications saved more than 100 pounds. After all

There was plenty of Pontiac performance success to go around as this 1962 Hurst ad shows.

Who says these old Pontiac lightweights still weren't racing long after they were built? Here, a factory lightweight 1962 Catalina gets down the track in 1991.

P.J. Heck

this lightening, the Catalina still weighed in at 3,600 pounds.

A number of former owners and drivers of the 1962 Super Duty quickly assured this was not the machine for the weak of heart. It quite simply was NOT a street car in any sense of the word. It had a rough idle, poor cold-running performance, a low-hanging oil pan that offered poor ground clearance, an ear-piercing exhaust noise, and it gulped premium fuel.

It was available to the buying public, but who would want to buy such a machine for the street? It looked and ran great on national drag strips, but cruising around the drive-in, heading to work or driving to the local grocery didn't make this an ideal machine.

One of the most famous on the national drag circuit was another of Beswick's "Passionate Ponchos." The initial "Ponchos" were the

aforementioned 1960 and '61 S/Ds which he ran in the earlier years.

Beswick realized that the lighter higher-performance 1962 Super Duty, with its 421 power, would easily overpower the 389 S/D cars. Through Selzer Pontiac in Chicago, he ordered one, then waited for the car to be painted his characteristic Bristol Blue color. Then he hit the track.

After several weeks of racing, he realized he needed more performance so he turned to Ray Nichols of Highland, Indiana for a .060 overbored short block. Arnie reworked the cylinder heads to NHRA specs.

Beswick campaigned the "Passionate Poncho II" east of the Mississippi River, and even with

Below: *This '62 Super Duty Catalina had an aluminum front end with the exception of the grille divider and headlight panel.*

The Courtesy Ford Thunderbolt in 1960s racing action.

Jack Biel

Jim Wangers, in his '62 SD Catalina two-door sedan, runs against Dave Strickler at Indy Raceway Park in the 1962 NHRA Nationals.

Jim Wangers Collection

transmission problems, it was able to win consistently. There were times when one or two gears of his four-speed were not functional, but he often got to the finish line first!

In September of 1962, he took the car to US 19 Dragway in Albany, Georgia where he won the Super Stock Eliminator Class against top Super Stock drivers along with setting a new track record of 12.11 seconds. He also was a popular attraction at Yellow River Dragway near Atlanta.

It is estimated that this car could have won more races than any other car in national Super Stock competition racing. Whenever there was a Super Stock drag race paying a decent purse, you would likely see Beswick. He even raced on 1/8 mile and 1,000-foot strips. Today, Arnie has the word out that he wants to buy back his Pontiac if it can be found.

Another strong 1962 Super Duty Catalina was the "Black Whirlwind" of Frank Barnett and Arlen Vanke. The black convertible was powered by a 389 Super Duty with a single four-barrel carb. Its accomplishments included the winning of the Top

Stock (C/SA) Class at York, Pennsylvania, along with a National NHRA Record in that same class of 97.19 miles per hour.

Vanke also drove a trio of famous 1962 Catalinas, the "Tin Indian," "Tin Indian II," and "Tin Indian Too." There were two class wins at the NHRA Indy Nationals, a fastest E.T. in Stock Eliminator (SS/S) at Indy, and the setting of an NHRA A/S National Record.

A small number of 421 S/D engines were also installed in lightweight Tempest cars with great success. Lloyd Cox won the A/Factory Experimental Class at the 1962 NHRA Nationals. But that wasn't the only Tempest that scored nationally that season as Hayden Proffitt won the same class at the 1962 Winternationals.

During the 1962 season, with the upgraded 389 S/D, there was a complete domination of NASCAR's top division. Super Duty-powered Catalinas crossed the finish line one-two-three at the Daytona 500, and went on to win 30 of 52 Grand National events.

A 1962 Pontiac Catalina Super Duty is ready for action.

Mike Mueller

1963 Catalina Super Duty

Never standing still, and not realizing that 1963 would be the final Pontiac lightweight season, the company moved the engine program up a few more notches.

The 12.5-1 engine received much of the effort. It had new 980 Heads sporting bigger intake ports and bigger exhaust ports with a 12.5-1 compression ratio with cylinder heads that contained larger valves. The new McKellar solid lifter #11 cam along with higher-tension dual-valve springs were welcome additions. During the season, Pontiac also made available another high-riser intake that provided additional power and torque.

The company announced that the horsepower figure was now up to 410, but dyno testing showed the reading was probably much closer to 540 horses!

Both the four-speed T-10 and three-speed T85 three-speed transmissions were used in the 1963 Super Dutys. The T-10 had a couple low gear ratio options, an all-aluminum case and was up to 20 pounds lighter than the T-85, which had an aluminum tailshaft housing and a steel main case.

That was great stuff under the hood, but add that to the fact that the car had also shed about 40 additional pounds with the use of a Plexiglass windshield. More weight was removed at the company by excising portions of the perimeter frame rails, turning tube sections into channel sections.

The use of aluminum pieces obviously bought the desired lightening, but just a lean on an aluminum fender could damage it seriously. A number of the top teams reverted back to sheet metal. It was not strange to see signs warning "Aluminum, do not touch."

"You can practically dent the fenders with your thumb," *Hot Rod* columnist Roger Hunnington wrote in a 1963 Pontiac feature. "A lot of weight has been taken out of the exhaust system. The cast aluminum split-flow, dual outlet headers are now being installed as standard equipment."

Several other goodies were available to further reduce weight with aluminum bumper attachment parts, splash pans, and radiator core supports. The wildest of the weight-reducing modifications were made to less than a dozen Catalinas. They underwent what was the so-called "Swiss Cheese" modification.

Those particular Catalinas had the look of the famous cheese with unbelievably large holes drilled in the frame rails. It certainly saved, but there was always a safety concern about the removal of that much metal from a frame member. Some of those "Swiss Cheese" cars suffered large wrinkles in the quarter panels before it was determined some frame beef-up was necessary.

Other aluminum substitutions in the Swiss Cheese machines included the outer and inner fender wells, a differential carrier, alternator bracket, and the bumper brackets. The aluminum was thinner than the 1962 S/D version—only 26 gauge. Pontiac didn't forget anything in their weight-trimming exercise.

In addition, there was the expected radio and heater delete, and removal of body sealer, insulation, and sound deadening. The battery was also in the right-side trunk location to increase rear weight. Overall weight savings was recorded as 330 lbs. from the 1962 version.

The cars were still considerably heavier than the Super Stock Plymouths and Dodges. Those cars

The 1963 Royal Pontiac Catalina is shown in action that year at the Detroit Dragway.

Jim Wangers Collection

A 1963 Pontiac 421 SD is getting ready to run.

had unibody construction and were several hundred pounds lighter.

One aspect of the Swiss Cheese machines was the modification negated the model from participating in the high-profile Super Stock Class. These cars were required to participate in the Factory Experimental (FX) Class. The 1963 Catalinas with all the reduction options in place weighed in at about 3,325 pounds.

The top Pontiac drivers got them, including Beswick, Arlen Vanke of Knafel Pontiac, Thompson, and Royal Pontiac. Another went to the Van Winkle Pontiac dealership in Dallas, Texas. Beswick explained he had to buy his "Swiss Cheese" machine while others were more fortunate getting a dealer to acquire one for them.

Van Winkle general manager Monk King used Pontiacs for advertising. He helped the legendary Smokey Yunick to achieve wins with NASCAR. That particular Catalina was run in the southwest U. S. and has since been restored back to its former configuration.

Guess it's not surprising to learn that Beswick's '63 Swiss Cheese Lightweight was coined the "Passionate Poncho III." With that car and the other just-mentioned drivers, Beswick tore up the drag sport during 1963.

The Passionate Poncho III was painted in a Fire Mist gray, as all the "Swiss Cheese" cars were. In Arnie's case, black and blue lettering shaded with red proclaimed his nickname, "The Farmer" across the doors.

Vanke was on the scene again with his "Swiss Cheese" 1963 Catalina. The "Tin Indian III" set a track record at Quaker City Dragway in Ohio of 12.26 seconds and 115.78 miles per hour.

Another lightweight 421 S/D Catalina ran uphill at the Pikes Peak Hill Climb, driven by Johnny Maruo. The car, which has been displayed at the Floyd Garrett Museum, was the final 1963 Super Duty of the run of 85 cars. The engine carried a single Carter 625-cfm carb and had a rating of 390 horses. Only a single-carb version was allowed for that big hill.

The car had a lightweight treatment that included aluminum bumpers, inner and outer fenders, the hood and its bracings, valance, and radiator core support. But there was no "Swiss Cheese" holes and the Pontiac weighed some 3,700 pounds.

Also in 1963, 13 Super Duty Tempests were constructed. There were reportedly seven LeMans Coupes and six station wagons that received the 421 S/D engine, though other figures are floating around.

Pontiac was serious about going racing in the early 1960s, and thought the super light Tempests with that 421 S/D under the hood was just too much of a temptation to pass up. Both the Tempest wagons and coupes, in addition to the 421 S/D engine, had aluminum front sheet metal making the already light vehicles even more desirable.

The clutch-operated four-speed transaxle automatic they carried placed more weight over the rear axle and allowed for clutchless shifting, somewhat similar to the Lenco drag transmissions on modern Pro-Mod and Pro Stock cars.

There were problems that resulted in the 3.90 ratio ring gear being replaced frequently. And since it was the lowest gear ratio that would fit, some teams replaced the entire transaxle.

The Super Duty Tempests were built over the Christmas holidays of 1962, and delivered just prior

A restored 1963 "Swiss Cheese" Pontiac SD.

Tom Glatch

to the March 1963 GM corporate racing ban. Beswick got one of each, and campaigned them with his '63 "Swiss Cheese" Catalina. Beswick coined the coupe "Little B's Runabout" that he bought from Mickey Thompson and the station wagon he named "The Grocery Getter."

The coupe was raced through the 1965 season, match racing and competing in Super Stock and A/FX shoot-outs across the country. The "Grocery Getter" name was declared by the announcer at a race to have "Taken home the groceries again" after several consecutive wins.

In Chicago, Arnie was racing at the International Amphitheater, where cars raced the length of the building, then exited through two garage doors before slowing down in an adjoining building. The original wagon passed through several owners after Arnie and its present location is unknown.

The coupes did well in competition with Lloyd Cox and Hayden Proffitt behind the wheel. There was much match racing and also some Super Stock competition at national events.

Arlen Vanke was also a tear in one of the LeMans Coupe lightweights, the "Running Bear." It set an A/FX National Record of 11.89 seconds/123.28 miles per hour in Alton, Illinois. Vanke also had one of

the Tempest wagons, the "Papoose One" that won many local and regional events. Another driver with the Knafel Pontiac team that 1963 season was Bill Abraham in the "Golden Arrow." He won the Indy Nationals with a 13.28-second, 109.48 mph effort.

The boss man at Knafel was Bill "Tin Indian" Knafel and his Pontiac lightweights were a dominant force in Super Stock racing. From 1959 through 1971, his 32 Pontiacs won more than 200 national and world races.

"We had an engineering capability at our dealership where we reworked everything," Bill explained. "I accepted more cars right out of Pontiac's Engineering Department than anyone else. The cars would come off the assembly line and we would be there to pick them up."

Pontiac honcho John DeLorean sent Knafel a 1963 Tempest for road tests and Knafel quickly made some alterations for drag racing. That would become the aforementioned "Running Bear."

In a June 1963 story about the Tempests, *Hot Rod* magazine reported that stock car drivers formed an alliance against the powerful Tempests. And they fit under NHRA weight limits as well.

"Total car weight is in the vicinity of NHRA's legal minimum of 7.5 pounds per cubic inch which figures out about 3,160 for the 421 engine" said *Hot Rod*. "We have seen a few of these Tempests in action on the drag strip and they are real terrors. When the power is turned on they don't even spin a tire, they just go."

The General Motors factory competition ban had a chilling effect on the Pontiac Division in particular according to the article.

"It looks as though Pontiac management had some real serious plans about dominating the Super Stock division at the drags before somebody in a higher position put the lid on performance," *Hot Rod* reported. "…we can't say that we blame the boys driving other brands for staying away from the starting line when one of these 'compacts' is getting ready to run."

Acquiring the Coveted S/D Parts

There were actually early-vintage Super Duty parts sold over the counter as early as 1960. They helped make Pontiac a powerhouse by the early 1960s as evidenced by accomplishments both on the drag strips and oval tracks.

By late 1961 and early 1962, the parts or cars could be special ordered when either a Grand Prix or Catalina was ordered at the dealership. That was the same situation with the 1963 S/D models that culminated this glorious factory lightweight era for Pontiac.

Today, the value of the Super Duty cars from this era is truly mind-boggling. If one of the famous lightweight models, in restored condition, is placed on the auction block, it's not unlikely that it could bring into the six-figures! If the car had a famous driver, it might double in value. Who would ever have guessed, as several muscle car experts indicated, that these cars could be purchased for just hundreds of dollars in the 1970s and 1980s!

General Motors Says No More Racing

It was an amazing turn of events. The publicity and sales that Pontiac achieved from its lightweight drag machines was unbelievable. But in March 1963, the corporate fist hit the table. The companies had made such an agreement in 1957, but it was ignored. The 1963 manufacturer's ban effectively ended continuous improvement on the Super Duty and high performance programs. Had the program continued, there was the possibility of extensively upgrading the 421 S/D engine with a single overhead cam configuration.

As soon as there was a hint that the ban was coming, a number of the "Swiss Cheese" cars were rushed to completion. There were reportedly about two truck-loads of S/D parts and pieces that were disseminated to the Pontiac dealers that were supporting the race teams.

There were a handful of independent Super Duty Pontiacs that had been built before the ban, and there was some success with those cars. They soon lost their edge due to the lack of availability of replacement Super Duty parts.

The Tempests gave new meaning to Pontiac lightweight drag racing.
Mike Mueller

PONTIAC MUSCLE:
Before the GTO

As advertising proclaimed "America's Number One Road Car" in 1957 and "The Wide Track from Pontiac" in 1959, the Pontiac Division of General Motors was redefining itself as a true performance car.

It started in 1957 under the direction of Simon "Bunky" Knudsen who planned to alter Pontiac's stuffy image. Racing and performance received attention as Knudsen hired race car performance engineer Ray Nichels.

"I worked directly under Knudsen," Nichels recalled in *High Performance Pontiac.* "I'd meet with the engineering department. We even had access to the metallurgists. They were always willing to help improve things."

Soon Nichels prepared a '57 Chieftain for the Winter Grand Nationals at Daytona Beach, Florida. Cotton Owens drove the Pontiac to a win and Nichels became even more involved in Pontiac motorsports.

Meanwhile, Pontiac offered the

public a limited edition Bonneville convertible. It looked great and could go 130 mph. Pontiac began to knock the socks off the car buying public and became *the* car to have at the track.

In 1958, just enough NASCAR certified Tempest 395-A V-8s were made to attract attention to Pontiac. This engine could produce 300 hp with the proper carbs, heads, cams and camshaft. And a powerful Pontiac Bonneville led the competitors at the Indianapolis 500 on May 30, 1958.

By 1959, Pontiacs became the terrors of NASCAR and USAC tracks and began to be a presence at drag strips as well. One of the

The 1958 Pontiac Bonneville convertible led the pack at the Indianapolis 500.

The 1958 Pontiac Bonneville Sport Coupe created more excitement.

first Pontiac drag racing successes was a 1959 Knafel Pontiac station wagon that won the New York State Championship in the Super Stock class.

In 1960, driving with hand controls, wheelchair-bound drag racer Earl Rowe of Richmond, Virginia, placed second by just 10 points in competition for the Top Ten world championship of drag racing in his new Pontiac Wide Track screamer.

In 1961, Joe Weatherly and Paul Goldsmith captured the NASCAR and USAC championships in Nichels-prepared Pontiacs. The cars continued to make a name on the drag strips across the country and the

In 1961 and '62, the Pontiac Super Duty challenged all comers on drag strips and oval tracks.
Mike Mueller

The 1963 Pontiac Super Duty continued the division's performance path.

Mike Mueller

public pushed Pontiac into third place in sales.

The Knafel team, and Royal Oak Pontiac team were among those who achieved drag racing success with 1962 Pontiac lightweights.

Aluminum body parts, a revised 405-hp 421-cid engine and a weight in the 3,000-pound range helped send many Ponchos down the strip to cross the finish line in first place. The Super Duty Catalina meant Pontiac had arrived as *the* car to race.

Arlen Vanke drove three versions of the Knafel 421 Super Duty Catalinas and set various records or won prestigious titles like the Indy Nationals. Also, a Catalina convertible nicknamed the "Black Whirlwind" added to the Vanke/Knafel list of achievers winning the Top Stock C/SA class with an NHRA record speed of 97.19 mph.

Pontiac continued to improve its 1963 edition of the Super Duty Catalina

boosting horsepower to an official 400. Those in the drag racing know said it was actually in the 540 to 550-hp range in strip prep.

The curtain officially closed on factory-sponsored Pontiac racing in May 1963 but Arnie Beswick continued to win with two mid-sized Tempest lightweight screamers.

It was the end of a great era for Pontiac's official racing sponsorship. Once the ban was in effect, oval track racer Goldsmith moved on

Bold new advance in V-8 efficiency

TEMPEST 395

Command the jeweled-action response of the most efficient V-8 of all time. Choose from four power options available for any Golden Jubilee Pontiac model to match your own kind of driving!

270 HP	285 HP	TRI-POWER	FUEL INJECTION
Twin-barrel carburetor, 10:1 compression ratio. Standard on Chieftains	Four-barrel carburetion, 10:1 compression ratio. Standard on Star Chief	Twin-range response gives you both two-barrel economy and six-barrel per-	310 horsepower, 10.5:1 c.r.; the ultimate in re- sponse, operating econ-

Above: *Before it was a Pontiac model, the Tempest was a performance V-8 engine.*

to Chrysler. Weatherly soon joined Mercury.

"The Farmer" Beswick kept the Pontiac candle burning on the drag strip.

Midway in the 1964 model year, the GTO option package was promoted for the Tempest Le Mans. The popularity of the GTO would bring the public and stock and drag racers to Pontiac in waves that Nichels, Knudsen and others could never have imagined in 1957.

The era of the muscle-clad Pontiac tiger was just beginning as the racing glory faded.

Left: *Arlen Vanke took the new Tempest to several wins during the 1963 season.*

Bob Plumer

Trying to Carry On

Only Beswick and dealer Gay Pontiac continued to field Pontiacs on a professional level. Most of the other Pontiac professional racers turned to Ford and Chrysler since both companies still supported drag racing.

Beswick machines still won just about everything during 1963, garnering events like The World Series of Drag racing, the NASCAR Daytona Winternationals, and the much-coveted *Drag News* Invitational. Beswick explained that he used the equipment that he already had in his possession and was lucky that he didn't have any major breakdowns.

For the 1964 season, Beswick purchased a new GTO coupe and converted it into a supercharged, nitro-fueled, non-altered wheelbase A/FX (and later S/FX) machine known as "The Mystery Tornado." Initially, the Tornado carried a 421 S/D power plant with a pair of four-barrel carbs.

"But with the 'no holds barred' rules of the drag race sport at that time, I decided to go with the blower and nitro, as all the other brands were also doing." Arnie continued. "There was no factory support or parts available, but I was fortunate that my GTO came with an aluminum front end. The car was also a radio and heater delete. It ended up weighing about 3,250 pounds, and it was capable of outrageous performance."

Two Pontiac lightweight heavy hitters, Jim Wangers (left) and Arnie Beswick, joke at a Pontiac Performance meet at the Norwalk Dragway in Ohio in 2004.

Arnie Beswick is one of the few original lightweight drivers who still participates in current events. He's shown next to the replica of one of his former cars.

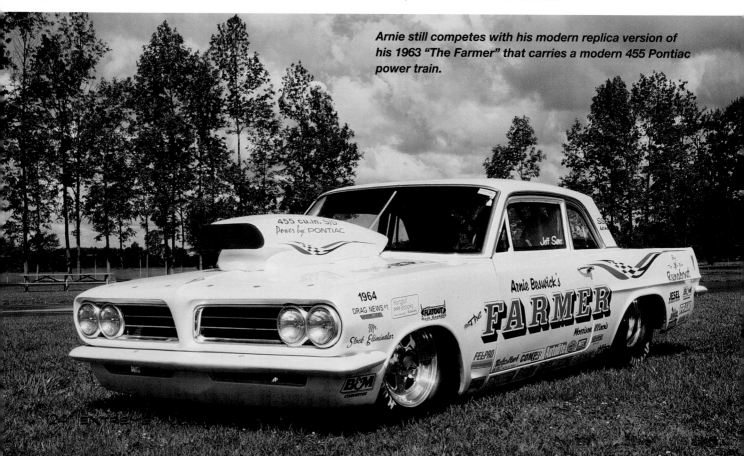

Arnie still competes with his modern replica version of his 1963 "The Farmer" that carries a modern 455 Pontiac power train.

The famed Beswick fiberglass GTO races in night action.

Bob Plumer

Reportedly, it was the first car to drop into the nine-second range. Later that year it dropped into the eight-second performance regimes.

"A majority of the events we participated in were match and S/FX races across the country. We put on some great shows and were much in demand by the fans and track operators. There were so few GM cars racing at the time, we brought out the fans who were tired of watching just Fords and Mopars."

Beswick continued to run the 1963 wagon and 421 S/D Catalina during the 1964 season. He then went to the Daytona Beach Winternationals and ran against all the 1964 cars from Ford and Chrysler. During the six nights of racing, he won every race

with the coupe. The wagon and Catalina also won their classes.

In 1966, Beswick maintained his Pontiac allegiance by driving a new lightweight fiberglass-bodied GTO. In 1967, Beswick put his old '63 LeMans coupe back in service as an S/FX supercharged Factory Experimental. It was painted in a garnish orange and black striped motif and was called the "Tameless Tiger."

If looks could kill, this would have been a dreaded giant. The LeMans-based dragster still carried all its lightweight components. It had a modern look with a low-hanging front spoiler and a modern-looking blower and fuel injection hood scoop.

The "Star of the Circuit" Beswick GTO leaves the line in a mid-1960s drag race.

The ever-present 421 S/D engine was still doing its thing under the hood, hooked to a Turbo400 automatic transmission and a 1961 Pontiac rear end. The first time it hit the track, it turned impressive low nine-second clockings and later dropped into the eights.

The 1966 season was dynamite for the Knafel team with a pair of 389 Tri-Power GTOs chauffeured by Vanke, Abraham, and "Doc" Dixon. There were numerous championships won that unbelievable season in the "Tin Indian V" machines.

The wins included winning the NASCAR Winternationals and NHRA Spring Nationals. The remainder of the decade saw success in a 1966 LeMans Convertible, a 1967 Acadian (a Chevelle and Chevy II-based "cousin" from the Canadian GM Pontiac Division), and a 1968 GTO Ram Air II 400. Dixon would be the driver much of the time.

Also during the 1966 season, Knafel brought out the "Mystery Tornado II" with Vanke at the wheel. This Tempest was a convertible with an overhead cam six-cylinder. The ragtop was the I/S Champion at the NASCAR Winternationals and held IHRA records in the I/S and J/S Classes.

In late 1967, with Arnie Behling driving, the original Tiger LeMans Coupe was crashed and destroyed at Winston-Salem, North Carolina. Only a few parts were saved.

Beswick debuted an amazing 1966 GTO drag machine called the "Star of the Circuit" for the late 1966 and 1967 seasons. Many considered it the most beautiful General Motors products to ever hit the drag racing scene. The car used a stock 1964 GTO frame with a lightweight Logghe tubular front axle and a stock-dimension lightweight fiberglass 1966 GTO body.

Power for this car came from a 428 supercharged and fuel-injected nitro-fueled Pontiac engine that was set further back about 25 percent for better weight distribution. It weighed in at a lean 3,050 pounds.

This Pontiac was a real fan favorite as he mostly competed in the popular match racing during this time period. The first time down the track, the Beswick GTO turned an impressive 8.59-second E.T. at 167 miles per hour in the NHRA S/FX Class.

In 1968, Beswick built an unnamed GTO-based dragster and was similar looking to the 1966 version. Weighing less than the '66 model, it had a one-piece flip-top body. Of significance was the fact that it was Arnie's first e-frame chassis. Capable of running in the eights and high sevens, the car was vigorously match-raced.

"It, however, had a solid-mount rear end," says Beswick. "That made the car unpredictable in starting line performance, frequently making a hard right or left turn.".

Knafel came on again during the period with a pair of Dixon-Driven "Tin Indians," one a 1967 427-powered Acadian from Canada Pontiac that won the AHRA B/Modified Championship. Another was a 1968 GTO Ram Air II 400 that set an AHRA D/S World Record.

In 1969, the Beswick race team performance was shining brightly with the advent of three similarly-painted GTO Judges. The slowest machine, called "The Judge" used a factory Ram Air IV power plant and raced in the D Stock Class. It was one of the few radio/heater and deadener/insulation delete factory cars.

In addition, there was a flip-up fiberglass-front, steel bodied Judge called the "Righteous Judge," followed by the ultimate lightweight machine, the so-called "Super Judge." This was a complete Logghe

The 1966 "Star of the Circuit" GTO S/FX carried a fiberglass GTO body with a supercharged nitro-burning 421 SD power plant.

tubular-frame, fiberglass front flip-up/steel bodied machine that ran in the 1969 Super Stock Nationals where he had a best effort of 7.89 seconds. It was his first from-scratch professionally-built race car.

The blown and injected 428-cid Pontiac engine was attached to a Turbo 400 tranny and a Pontiac big car rear end. Arnie thought he had might be able to get some sponsorship from the Chicago-Area Pontiac Dealers Association, but it fell apart when Pontiac decided to drop the availabilityof high performance engines. Since the public couldn't by the engines, the dealers association decided it didn't make sense to sponsor a high-performance car. Arnie indicated he team didn't get the sponsorship because GM had dropped all performance engine development because of 1969 emission requirements.

Below: *Jim Wangers attempted to revive the Pontiac high performance image after General Motors dropped its support in 1963. He used a pair of "GeeTO Tiger!" GTOs like this replica.*

The GeeTO Pontiacs

One person who took the killing of Pontiac in motor sports to heart was Pontiac advertising agency employee and top lightweight Pontiac driver, Jim Wangers.

"The Super Duty program along with the many wins we had in the early 1960s were great assets to selling cars. The advent of the GTO, though, which had Pontiac lightweight roots, brought

Pontiac performance back in the limelight," he explained.

Wangers decided to instigate a program with several GTOs that were gaudily painted with the "GeeTO" name covering the sides. The Wangers plan promoted the cars from drag strip to drag strip, match racing and reminding fans Pontiac still had performance even though it was no longer allowed to build any lightweight cars or high-performance engines.

Today, Wangers has resurrected the old "GeeTO" Tiger Mystic with replicas of one of his most-famous GTOs.

Chapter 8

OFF-SHOOT
LIGHTWEIGHTS

O.K. So this whole book has involved itself with the advantages on the drag strip of weighing less. The performance gains were definitely amazing during those days.

But there have been other applications of this phenomenon. Not nearly as well publicized is the fact there were also attempts to achieve the same effect in stock car racing. And in a long-range durability run during that 1960s time period, the test cars were lightened to ease the stress to the power train.

Also, during the 1970s, there was another lightweight effort that was strictly non-performance. Several production models were given an aluminum treatment for increased fuel economy.

It was a great idea, but didn't seem to catch on.

Even during the 1970s there were several additional lightweight drag efforts. And finally, there might have been one other Big-Three Division that might have also had lightweight drag participation, but it never made it. Interested? Read on!

Grand American Comet Stock Car

Bud Moore was well known in NASCAR circles as an innovator, with much of his magic being performed with Ford. In 1966, he took a new Comet Cyclone and performed some major lightening.

NASCAR owner Bud Moore accomplished major lightening on this 1966 Comet stock car by modifying the front end. Driven by Darrel Derringer, it is currently owned by David Tom.

David Tom Collection

Pit crews work on Richard Petty's #43 Plymouth during the 1964 racing season.

Phil Hall Collection

The first effort was when he discovered that the Mercury had double thickness sheet metal in the shock towers and radiator support. Bud figured that he could fabricate a completely rigid front end for the car by strategically placing tubing within the front portion of the stock chassis. That resulted in a lighter front end for the car, therefore gaining a better front-to-rear weight distribution.

1964 MOPAR Stock Car Package

Granted, Chrysler had a huge interest in its Super Stock drag program, but it also addressed the stock car program. For the 1964 model year, there was a track option package called the A864. It provided minimal weight saving with an aluminum intake manifold, aluminum K-head valve covers, and an aluminum-cased four-speed transmission.

In their racing predictions for the 1964 season, *Motor Trend* quoted NASCAR veteran driver and Plymouth team leader Lee Petty. His words were prophetic.

"The new Plymouth should be a little better suited to the high-speed tracks like Daytona. It's more streamlined than the '63 model and the new 426-inch engine should be stronger and lighter."

In May 1964, *Motor Trend* reacted to the Mopar success at Daytona where Plymouths finished one through three and a Dodge was fifth.

"Last February, the best Plymouths and Dodges, including Richard Petty's, struggled around Daytona at 150 mph and less. This time," noted *M/T* "all the new ones easily topped 170 mph and were officially clocked as high as 174.910 which earned Paul Goldsmith pole position."

Most of the cars arrived with both radio and heater delete and removal of all four headlights, which provided a substantial weight savings. Many of these MOPAR haulers also ran without their wheel covers.

A 1964 Plymouth on a NASCAR oval. It was a very successful season for the Mopars.

The Mercury Comet stock car shared its racing image with the Cougar and Cyclone on a 1968 Super Stock cover.

Plymouth was proud of its new image in this 1964 ad.

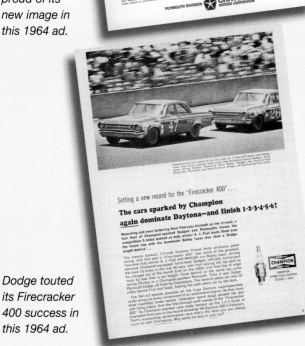

Dodge touted its Firecracker 400 success in this 1964 ad.

The Plymouths and Dodges won several races in 1964 including finishing first and second at the World 600 (both Plymouths) where Bobby Isaac's Dodge had led for large portions of the race.

At the Firecracker 400, Richard Petty captured the lead from pole sitter and Mercury driver Darel Dieringer on the first lap and headed the pack for long periods in the race.

Winner A. J. Foyt gushed about his Dodge power plant after the race.

"…Chrysler's new hemi-head engines put Plymouths and Dodges in a class by themselves."

At the Southern 500 at Darlington, South Carolina, Buck Baker brought his '64 Dodge home a winner, the first time a Chrysler-made car had won the Southern 500 since its first year, 1950, when Johnny Mantz took the crown in his Plymouth.

It was that way all season and in 1965, NASCAR changed the rules, forcing Chrysler to homologate its engines and, in effect, sidelined them. But they were back in 1966. By then, the Hemi already was a legend and Chrysler cars had a great reputation on the strip as well as the oval tracks.

1963 421 Pontiac Tempest Stock Car

For the 1963 season, Pontiac introduced a new lightweight Tempest stock car with aluminum sheet metal, 54 percent rear end weight, and weighing only 3,200 pounds.

The few manufactured got their share of attention. Under the hood was the ever-so-familiar 421 SD power plant with a 420-horse rating.

One difference from the 1963 Super Stock drag cars was that these machines used a cast iron manifold, rather than aluminum. The cars came in both coupes and station wagons. From the firewall rearward, the body was standard but ahead of this dividing line, aluminum was the name of the game. Inner and outer fender panels, hood radiator, bumper and miscellaneous brackets were all fabricated of the light metal.

One of the notable Tempests was one prepared by the Ray Nichels Garage in Highland, Indiana and driven by Paul Goldsmith. In the 250-mile NASCAR Challenge Cup race, the Goldsmith Tempest drove away from the competition.

Nichels' mechanics attached a lightweight aluminum bracket to the rear A-frame, then mounted a power steering pump with a belt drive from the pulley on the right swing axle to circulate oil between the transaxle unit and radiator. Stuffing the large 421 engine into the Tempest engine bay did call for some creative engineering.

"Since the Tempest uses a transaxle unit with the transmission in the rear, Pontiac engineers decided to gain more room for the left manifold by moving the starter motor and flywheel to the transaxle unit," reported *Hot Rod* writer Ray Brock in June 1963.

The transmission mated a pair of two-speed TempesTorque automatics, added between the rear axle and the torque converter.

"We have seen a few of these Tempests in action on the drag strip and they are real terrors," wrote Brock. "These cars seem to have little trouble getting under the 12-second elapsed time mark and speed runs well over 120 mph for the quarter."

A 1962 Tempest lightweight A/FX test car. Was it ever raced in competition?

Comet accomplished a 100,000 mile durability test with some of its 1964 cars.

The article was headlined "The Tempest That Could Have Been King," an appropriate title for the little stocker that averaged 145.161 mph at the 250-mile Challenge Cup race at the 1963 Daytona International Speedway's Speedweek.

1964 Comet 100,000 Mile Car

It was an advertising effort of performance and durability that had never been accomplished before. It involved an attempt by Ford to run one hundred thousand miles at over one hundred miles per hour. The Daytona International Speedway, with its 31-degree banking was the site of the attempt over four decades ago.

Four Mercury Comets were prepared for the Herculean task. The machines were equipped with the brand new Comet Cyclone 289-cubic inch high-performance power plant equipped with a four-barrel carb, mechanical lifters, custom cams, and alternators.

It didn't take long to prove that these little hot rods were up to the task. Records were cracked all along the way until the lead car completed 101,594 miles at an unbelievable 108+ miles per hour on

David Pearson's 1971 Mercury Cyclone in NASCAR action.

October 30, 1963. In all, there were over 100 world records for speed and distance, plus dozens of American records.

Lightening up the cars was accomplished with removal of the second front seat and the back seat. The trim panel was pulled along with deletion of the radio and heater. Finally, there was a unique fiberglass gas tank.

"One of the specially-equipped Comets completed a 10,000 mile run at an average of 124.421 mph to shatter the international Class C record, the national Class C record and the American unlimited record for closed cars for the distance," reported *Motor Trend.*

The cars were powered by the new Mercury Cyclone 289-cid V-8 with four-barrel carbs Inside were mechanical valve lifters and a high performance cam. The Comets had stiffened suspensions, used heavy duty axles and drive shafts.

The Comets ran over 40 straight days, from Sept. 21 through Oct. 30, 1963.

"Hour after hour, night and day, through humid heat and tropical storms brewed by hurricanes

One of the first ads that touted the 100,000 mile Comets from January 1964.

This is one of the specially-prepared 1964 Comets used in the Comet 100,000 mile Durability Run—100,000 miles at 100 miles per hour.

Comet referred to its endurance run when the Cyclone was introduced later in 1964.

Flora and Ginny, the Comets chalked up more than 2,500 miles each day," said the *M/T* account.

"Several times the Comets skidded in the rain-slicked pavement, spun out, and continued—with or without damage—around the race track."

Hot Rod carried a Lincoln-Mercury-supplied account of the durability run that talked about the pounding the engines took.

"The crankshaft made 204 million revolutions. Each valve spring, valve, rocker arm, pushrod and tappet cycled 102 million times. Each piston traveled 18,524 miles, or the equivalent of six trips from New York to Los Angeles. Each carburetor metered out 11.5 million cubic feet of air."

The Daytona International Speedway marathon was actually one of three durability tests the Comets ran that fall. The first was a rugged 40,000-mile test at Romeo, Michigan, that Mercury engineers felt was comparable to 100,000 miles of rough roads, gravel and hills. A second run was over the potholes and cobblestones of the Dearborn, Michigan, Ford Proving Grounds.

In the spring of 1964, three Comet teams raced in the rugged African Safari through jungle, bush country and mountain roads.

Two teams finished, with the top team led by eight-time African Safari rally driver Viscount Kim Mandeville and his sidekick Peter Walker. At one point, their car and the Comet driven by Joginder and Jaswant Singh had to make it over a jerry-rigged bridge that had been washed out.

Hot Rod writer Ray Brock drove a third Comet rally car that did not finish but reported on the race in depth in the June 1964 issue and concluded this way.

"Any American automobile manufacturer who's looking for the toughest conditions in the world has to try Kenya, Uganda and Tanganyika. If you were to combine the worst features of all the proving grounds owned by Ford, Chrysler and General Motors…you'd never be able to equal one quick trip over the sections of road near Tambach and Mbulu."

Both the 100,000-mile tests and the African Rally were publicized in Comet advertising through the 1964 model year and well into the 1965 edition of the cars.

Charles Crites owns one of those long-range Comets and he's restored it back to its Daytona configuration. He's had the car since 1966. "The dealer had gotten the car from Mercury to display in his dealership. I only paid $425 for it, and drove it home."

Lightweight Production Models

In the mid-1970s, the lightweight phenomenon reared its head again when two lightweight production models were released by Chrysler. Obviously, the lightweight aspect of these models wasn't performance, but fuel economy. These now-rare 1976 models were known as the Plymouth Feather Duster and Dodge Dart Lite.

The models were constructed with an aluminum inner hood, trunk bracing, bumper brackets, and intake manifold. In addition, there was a fuel-sipping carburetor and precise distributor calibration. The engine economy effort continued with a large free-flowing exhaust system, a tall rear axle ratio, and either a three- or four-speed overdrive manual transmission.

The overall effect was immediate and for the time period the gas mileage was out-of-sight with up to 36 miles per gallon on the highway. Unfortunately, very few sold because they had to compete with the stylish new Aspen and Volare models.

The 1976 Plymouth Feather Duster was an economy-minded lightweight. Phil Hall Collection

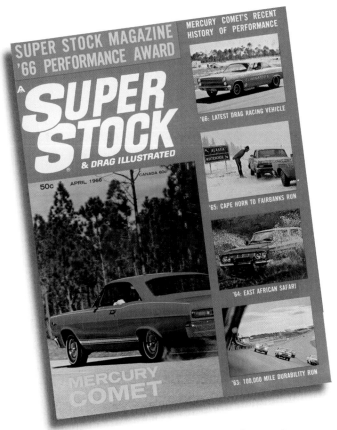

The April 1966 cover of Super Stock shows Comets in several durability tests. Phil Hall Collection

Chapter 9

LIGHTWEIGHT
MEMORIES

It's hard to imagine after all these years that the interest and charisma of the Lightweight drag scene is still with us. For a time after they went away in the late 1960s, there was practically zero interest in the unique drag machines.

But that's all changed with that era coming storming back with many that weren't even born when it happened. For many, it is so very hard to believe that cars such as these machines had such a factory connection. Guess it goes without saying that it will never happen again!

This chapter will reveal some current memories of those super-light cars. You will be surprised how much there is!

Diecast Models

In recent years, diecast models have emphasized the lightweight '60s Super Stock machines. Some of the examples, all done in 1/18th scale, and the associated companies and distributors are as follows:

Georgia Marketing (GMPdiecast.com) has produced many diecast performance models in the past few years. One is the 1966 Ford Fairlane factory drag car that carries the lightweight fiberglass hood

Arnie Beswick's 1966 GTO is one of the Fairfield Mint diecast model cars.

New Release!

Over 160 Parts!

BESTSELLER!

Front hinged hood

Roll bar and racing seat

Wired V-8 behind windshield

Removable engine cover

Wild "tiger" paint job

Arnie Beswick - Drag Race King
1966 Pontiac GTO Funny Car
1:18 Scale - 12" Long

Now, you can own the most famous funny car ever. Arnie "the farmer" Beswick's flame belching 1966 GTO. So radical, Arnie had to drive this monster from the back seat! Check out the wild "tiger stripe" paint job. Lift the front hinged hood. Checkout the fully plumbed fuel tanks. Inspect the racing seat with genuine cloth harnesses and roll bar. Simply amazing! Order today! **LFQ** 1966 Pontiac GTO Funny Car 2 payments of $29.99 each

Fairfield Mint

Joe Cochran of Jamestown, Ohio, created this replica of a 1963 Tempest SD altered wheelbase car.

and 427 power plant. And would you believe that you can even remove the hub caps for that classic lightweight look!

The company has also produced models of two of "Ohio George" Montgomery's factory Mustangs. They include the famous "Mr. Gasket" and "Malco" lightweight Gasser drag cars.

Highway 61 is an active lightweight Diecast producer with a number of the more-famous models including the 1968 Dick Landy Dart, the 1965 Stiles & Stahl Plymouth Belvedere, the 1963 "Little B's Runabout" of Arnie Beswick, and Bill Shrewsberry's '63 Tempest 421 SD.

SUP is also a heavy participator with such diecast models as the 1968 Sox & Martin and primer black and grey Plymouth Barracudas, 1964 Dodge 330 "Mr. Norm Grand Spaulding" and "Red Light Bandit" models, among others.

The Fairfield Mint (www.fairfieldmint.com) has a small number, but very high quality lightweight diecasts, with its Arnie Beswick 1966 Pontiac GTO Funny Car and 1964 "Mystery Tornado" plus a 1963 Don Nicholson Z-11 Chevy Impala.

Some of the dealers and distributors for these lightweight products include REPLICARZ, Designs in Motion(www.designsinm. com), Mason Distributing, Super Car Collectables, Diecast Muscle Cars (Diecastmusclecars.com)

Lightweight Replicas

As you can see from the contents of this book, there were very few Lightweights produced during the 1960s. Today it's possible to produce a model that looks and drives just like the original. In some cases, they're even better.

Crites Restorations
13155 U.S. Highway 23
Ashville, Ohio   740-983-4777
(Critesrestorations.com)
Also the home of Litening Bolt Performance Products

If creating a Lightweight Ford replica is your bag, you must converse with Crites Restorations near Columbus, Ohio. The company has specialized in 1957 through 1979 Fords and Mercurys since 1983.

For purposes of this book, Crites Restorations has the fiberglass body pieces, engine conversion kits, and hundreds of other parts needed to convert your Fairlane, Cyclone, Galaxie, Mustang, Comet, or Falcon into a period A/FX or B/FX clone.

These replicas are so authentic and realistic they are often taken for the real thing. And when one of these Crites cars is auctioned off, it's amazing the kind of money they bring even though they are just clones of the real thing.

All the fiberglass parts and pieces are fabricated on-site. Some of those parts include bumpers, hoods, gas tanks, trunk lids, fenders, hood scoops, stone deflectors, and others. Crites also provides a number of aluminum period Ford parts.

Mopars by Mosher
(Mosher's Musclecar Motors)
Monrovia, California
(Moparsbymosher.com)

In Monrovia, California, the emphasis of Mopars By Mosher is obviously the Chrysler brand. Bob Mosher, son of the writer for TV's "Leave It to Beaver" and "Munsters" series explained that initially his business concentrated on 1966+ cars such as Challengers, Chargers, Roadrunners, Cudas and the like. But things changed.

"I declared that I would specialize only on the 1962-1965 Dodge and Plymouth B Body lightweight Super Stock style cars. Some people thought that

Mike Moore, a Pontiac lightweight fan from Beavercreek, Ohio, created this magnificent replica of the Jim Wangers "GeeTO" Tiger.

622 Motorsports is a collection of original and replica Ford lightweights that are exhibited throughout the country.

e were crazy as the demand for these cars was still somewhat scarce, but I liked them so much that I just didn't care. It had also occurred to me that these cars would be hot and command big bucks in the future," Mosher explained.

"For the past few years, we have seen the cars we do go for even more money than the popular 'matching numbers' muscle cars, with the demand for these cars going off the Richter Scale.

Now we restore original factory lightweight cars, but probably do as many clone restorations. Even the replicas are drawing huge money too."

Mosher continued that the average time to produce a complete vehicle is about ten months. "I think the detail we produce is as close as possible to the way they were."

"These are hand-built cars down to the last nut and bolt," he says. "We will keep producing these historical vehicles more for the love of the cars than the desire to get rich, as it also is a hobby."

Mosher's vehicles have been featured in such places as *MoPar Muscle*, *Popular Hot Rodding*, and *Hot Rod* magazine, among many others. You can also see examples at the Mosher Web site.

Greg Donohue Collector Car Restorations

12900 South Betty Road, Floral City
Florida 34436   352-344-4329
(gregdonohue.com)

Greg Donohue Collector Car Restorations Inc. has been in the business for over 30 years dealing exclusively in 1963 and 1964 full size Ford New Old

Stock and Reproduction parts and accessories.

Donohue has owned three different 1963-1/2 and 1964 Galaxie Lightweights along with restoring and supplying parts and technical advice to over 125 lightweight owners. His parts company can usually supply most of the unique or hard-to-find items for the Ford Lightweights or at least be able to tell you where you can locate them. He also handles all of the common restoration items you would need to restore or replicate one of these cars. Helpful diagrams and categories help restorers find what they're looking for.

The real Malco Gasser Mustang in a 1968 ad.

In business since 1972, Donohue is considered the leading supplier in the world for the '63 and '64 Ford. A leading Ford authority and national judge, he guarantees his parts and supplies.

"All the parts that are reproduced must be approved by Greg Donohue to his satisfaction both in design and fit before they are sold," says the Donohue information page.

Cloning Lightweights

Because of the small number of actual lightweights, there have been a huge number of replicas built. A vast majority of these cars are claimed to be clones by their owners, but once again, when you lay down big money for what you assume is the Real McCoy, be sure that you are getting what you are paying for.

Included in this book are two examples of lightweight replicas that have been built. The "Grocery Getter" replicates the historic machine of Arnie Beswick. The "Warrior" is a correctly-built lightweight, but it doesn't represent any of the former lightweights.

The "Grocery Getter"

One of the most interesting of the lightweight cars was a lightweight Pontiac Tempest Wagon driven by Arnie Beswick and called the "Grocery Getter." The original version of this dragster no longer exists, but there is a completed clone of the famous wagon.

There were only six such 1963 lightweight Tempest wagons built. With 421 power and lots of aluminum parts, the cars had a big weight advantage over the larger Catalinas. They also used a clutch operated four-speed transaxle that effectively allowed clutchless shifting. It was a very close call that these wagons even made it at all, being constructed just before the GM ban on racing came down.

Working with Arnie Beswick, who drove the real "Grocery Getter," three enthusiastic co-owners were involved. They included Ohioans Eric Larson, Mike Garblick, and the late Wayne Martin. They started the ambitious project in 1994. After talking to Arnie Beswick about the project, and getting his approval, the project began with Beswick

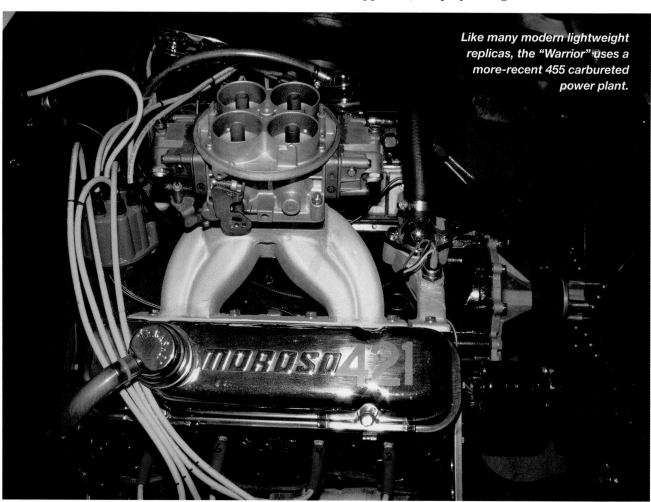

Like many modern lightweight replicas, the "Warrior" uses a more-recent 455 carbureted power plant.

giving them a spare 1963 Tempest wagon body as a starting point. When it was finished it was hard to tell the replica from the original. One reason was that the original painter, Jim Chandler, also lettered this clone.

"Our car hit the track for the first time in 1996 at Norwalk Raceway Park in Ohio," reported the Grocery Getter team's Web site. "We finished the weekend with a naturally-aspirated 9.90 E.T. at 135 mph. The next outing was the 1996 U.S. Nationals where we ran a series of exhibition runs culminating in a nitrous-assisted 8.90 E.T."

The car is a popular addition to major car events around the country and really attracts big crowds. Many are amazed that a station wagon actually performed in NHRA drag competition.

Garblick indicated that there had to be some changes made in the clone wagon, some required by modern safety rules. The original Getter didn't have a parachute as the clone vehicle has. Also, there is a more modern power train in place in the replica.

This Grocery Getter clone is NOT just a display vehicle. It has been run consistently since the mid-1990s. With the modern technology added, the best run for the GG clone is a heart-throbbing 7.82 seconds.

You are sure to see this stunning replica lightweight in many national Pontiac performance and drag race events.

The "Warrior"

Joe Cochran of Jamestown, Ohio is really hooked on the drag racing scene of the 1960s. His real passion, though, narrows down to the Altered Wheelbase Cars of the period. To that end, he built a clone of a 1963 lightweight Super Duty Tempest.

He explained, "I never intended from the beginning to fool anybody into thinking that this was the real thing. I tell everybody that I built it for my own enjoyment. The labor of love was completed in 1993, and the car has been competed a lot ever since."

The replica might look original on the outside, but Joe explained that he had modernized the clone in several ways. "But even though there is more performance from this car, I don't think it detracts from the nostalgic value of the machine," Cochran explained.

The actual Super Duty cars used the 421 Super Duty engines that were rated at 405 horsepower. Joe's machine carries those figures on his shaker

Ford performance expert Brent Hajek has a significant collection of performance machines.

hood and front quarters, but admits that he used a more readily-available 455-cid engine.

Filled with all the modern aftermarket pieces, Cochran said that his modern mill puts down about 600 horsepower.

The clone fulfills the A/FX name with an altered wheelbase configuration. "I moved the engine three inches further forward for better weight transfer, along with shortening the wheelbase by 14 inches."

Joe was able to get into the high nines at about 135 miles per hour with the clone, which compares with 11s at about 118 miles per hour for the originals. Besides the bigger horsepower numbers, the clone also has a Doug Nash five-speed transmission and a nine-inch Ford rear end by Mark Williams.

"The fans come out to see these cars race, but I really have to be careful that I don't overdo it. If you stand it up too high, you'll break something when you come down. If you don't go high enough, the fans aren't happy."

Lightweights in Collections

Even though the numbers of the lightweight cars were few in number, a large number of them still exist today. One place you can find them are in a number of performance car collections across the country.

The Rick Kirk Collection
6404 So. Ripley Road, Ripley
Oklahoma, 74062
918-372-4537

If there was ever a collector of all things vintage Ford performance that would have to be Rick Kirk of Ripley, Oklahoma.

The Ford Blue Oval is everything here, and that certainly includes a massive representation of lightweight Ford and Mercury equipment.

Included in the collection are a number of Lightweight Galaxies, a 1968 Cobra Jet Mustang, a 1965 B/FX Comet, period SOHC engines, and on and on.

A 1962 Ford Galaxie Lightweight greets visitors at the door with a sign that reports in large letters: "One of eleven built." The 1965 Comet has just 160 miles on the odometer and a legend that reports its makeup including fiberglass hood, doors, fenders and front bumper. It has its original tires, air lifts and plexiglass windshield and windows. Among other things, the Comet's sign notes the battery is in the trunk, there are factory-mounted traction bars and lightweight drag front seats also came from the factory.

Observed the Mothers® Hot Rod Power Tour in 2001: "All these cars are in 'as raced' condition. No over-restored trailer queens here. [Rick Kirk] is the greatest Ford guy I've ever met."

NHRA Museum
Fairplex Gate 1, 1101 W. McKinley Ave.
Pomona, California
909-622-2133

The Wally Parks NHRA Museum (museum.nhra.com) has a huge collection of vehicles plus photos, trophies and even helmets and uniforms that paint the story of the history of drag racing. The facility was opened in 1998 and is located in Pomona, California. There are a number of lightweight Super Stock cars on display. Admission is free to NHRA members and the museum is sponsored by the Automobile Club of Southern California.

Floyd Garrett's Muscle Car Museum
370 Winfield Dunn Parkway (Highway 66)
Sevierville, Tennessee 37876
865-908-0882
(www.musclecarmuseum.com)

Located in the small Tennessee town of Sevierville is the world-famous Muscle Car Museum of Floyd Garrett. Garrett is recognized as one of the national experts on the subject of vintage American muscle cars.

Included in that category are a number of the lightweight cars covered by this book.

You can see examples of both 1961 and '63 Pontiac Catalinas, a fastback Ford Galaxie from 1963, several Chevelles, Novas and Camaros, as well as many other fine cars.

In promoting Garrett's museum as a charter member of its Hall of Fame, *Muscle Car Review* wrote: "A spectacular landscape of wall to wall legends… All the great ones are here. Never have so many superb muscle cars been assembled under one roof."

Car Collector called the museum "…one of the finest collections of American muscle and stock car-based racing machines."

Could it be the "Little Old Lady from Pasadena's" red Super Stock Dodge? Mike Mueller

This well-done replica represents a 1968 Plymouth Barracuda lightweight drag car.

Brent Hajek Collection
Ames, Oklahoma

If you were to ask any performance Ford fan to name someone with the best of the Ford vintage performance toys, the name would flow with the name of Brent Hajek.

It all started in 1978 when Brent started becoming aware of Ford performance, in particular Ford drag racing machines.

"When I grew up, I loved watching the likes of Gas Ronda and Bob Glidden," Hajek explained.

From that time, the private collection began, and today, it numbers in the dozens, every one of them having a national reputation. Name most of the Ford lightweight cars of the 1960s, and you can bet that Brent has an example of many of them.

"That's the era that I really like, including the A/FX, Super Stocks, and Gassers of the period."

Not only does Hajek restore the cars, but he restores them to running condition and they are exercised at many national drag events.

Three of the Hajek cars, a Don Nicholson 1964 Comet, the "Lawman" '64 Plymouth driven by Al Eckstrand and Bob Glidden's 1980 Ford Fairmont were displayed at the NHRA Golden 50, a collection of the most famous NHRA dragsters in history at Indianapolis, Indiana.

Interviewed by the Enid, Oklahoma, *News and Eagle*, Hajek, who owns a trucking company and also is an oil and gas producer, observed: "There's never a dull moment. It's turned into a full-time job."

622 Motorsports
If you want to get up close and personal with Ford lightweight drag cars, the 622 Motorsports group is your answer.

This group appears at many Ford Motorsports events and brings a number of the lightweight cars that made history. In addition to the authentic cars, there are also a number of correctly-built replicas that are also on site. A number of the "real" lightweight drivers are also a part of the 622 show time.

Lightweights in National Events

The popularity of the 1960s lightweight machines is also typified by real and replica versions of the cars in many national events, including the MOPAR Nationals, Chrysler Classic events, Ford Expo Event, Super Chevy events, National Carlisle events, and numerous other.

There are also several organizations that concentrate strictly on these cars in competition. Among the most active is the National Street Car Association (NSCA). The group has actual competition events that feature Nostalgic Super Stock drag racing. All of the lightweight brands that ran in the 1960s are allowed, and they appear in either original or replica configurations. It's like stepping back four decades.

Chapter 10

LIGHTWEIGHT
SEEN ON THE STREET

There may never be another era quite like it. Factories were producing cars for the drag strip and racing ovals that weren't all that different from those available to racing wannabes down the street.

During the Lightweight Era, the distinctions between what was available on the street and what was being prepared for the strip were as razor thin as the aluminum fenders and fiberglass doors used to reduce weight.

In an era of racing success breeding sales success, the lightweight cars seen on the drag strips of the 1960s and early '70s were closely related to the cars seen in ads, in brochures and what drivers chose to buy.

Probably no other era blended the stars of the strip and the kings of the street so well together.

Throughout the decade, many cars dominated the drag racing scene and captured the attention of the driving public.

There were cars like the fire-breathing Pontiac Catalinas. Torque-twisting Chevrolets Z-11s. The powerful and rubber-burning Plymouths and Dodges. Muscular Mercurys. Fantastic Fords. The dynamic AMX and

While Pontiac was making a performance name on the strips and tracks, the Bonneville two-door hardtop was positioned as refined and urbane.

Ford's wildly popular 1965 Mustang 2 + 2 raised the bar a few notches. It was at home both as a lightweight drag racer or on the street scene.

David Lyon

Javelin.

While full sized cars were being drilled, stripped, tweaked and poked for weight loss potential, gas-sipping economy cars, introduced in the early 1960s, were quickly stuffed with the biggest engines possible and turned into lightweight terrors. Ford's Falcon, Mercury's Comet, the Chevy II and the Dart, Valiant and Barracuda, and others—all were converted to drag racing stars and quickly sprouted street muscle to accompany their strip fame.

In the mid 1960s, the practical mid-sized cars mushroomed, especially when Pontiac turned its exotic little Tempest into the GTO. Chevrolet's Chevelle, Ford's Fairlane and Torino, the Olds Cutlass, Buick Skylark and others quickly followed. Exploits on the drag strips were almost overshadowed by their street popularity. They quickly earned the tag "muscle cars."

And if all that wasn't enough, Ford took things a step further with its simple but revolutionary Mustang. Buyers could just about create any dream

they wanted with options and the performance minded quickly turned this pony into a thoroughbred. Mustang's popularity meant everyone followed and soon the Camaro from Chevrolet, the Firebird from Pontiac, Chrysler's new era Challenger, Mercury's Cougar and Plymouth 'Cuda and Dodge Challenger, as well as the AMX and Javelin, were on the street and being tooled for the strip.

During the lightweight era, if you didn't own a fire breather you probably lived next to someone who did, saw one in your town or neighborhood or were busy saving for a down payment to own one yourself.

These were cars of a generation, seen on the street, at high schools, in shopping centers or in traffic on the boulevard. While some were lucky enough to own one, many more wanted the cars of their dreams.

The discerning often knew the similarities and the parts that made these could make one of these cars into something really special. Everyone had ideas for making them even faster, wilder and more powerful. The cars seen on the street in the 1960s shared styling, engineering, prestige and parts with the cars that competed for a living on North American drag strips.

Even if they couldn't own the strip version of their favorite car, this new generation pushed for whatever came the closest to their dreams.

They would demand sexy looking cars with throaty-sounds and healthy boulevard bravado. Bucket seats, four speed or reliable automatic on the floor and a big engine under the hood all meant

something. Even if the Mustang or Chevy Impala SS or Road Runner was merely a daily driver, looks and lineage counted.

It was a time when anything seemed possible and the automakers and local dealers were only too eager to comply. Those with basic budgets or fat wallets all could step into something that made them feel like their car was something special.

Enterprising dealers like Bob Tasca in Rhode Island, Norm Kraus and Fred Gibbs in the Midwest, Bill Thomas in California and many others pushed

1960

Plymouth promised luxury, a low price and power in its Fury models like this 1960 convertible. *Phil Hall Collection*

Ford introduced new styling in 1960. The Galaxie Country Squire station wagon showed off the bold look . *Patrick Paternie*

1961

Above: *The Ford Starliner, new in 1960, received this beautiful styling in 1961.*
Phil Kunz

Right: *The 1961 Pontiac Bonneville Sports Coupe was refined but had a powerful racing heritage.*

The 1961 Chevrolet Impala Sports Coupe would star in SS and 409 trim but early on, it was part of the "Greatest Show on Worth."

Left: *You could see a lot of the USA in a 1962 Chevrolet Impala convertible, even more appealing in SS trim.* Phil Kunz

Lower Left: *Dodge emphasized economy and reliability in 1962 and many practical Darts like this one were seen long before a Pasadena granny got her Super Stock version.* David Lyon

Below: *It didn't get any more mainstream in 1962 than a new Mercury Monterey two-door hardtop parked out front of a beautiful new home.* Elton McFall Collection

While drag racers were thinking about the Z-11 version, many Chevrolet followers were lining up for the newly styled Corvette Sting Ray. Phil Kunz

5. Thunderbird 4-V/406 High-Performance V-8— 385 hp. Swift acceleration and top range output to please the most exacting performance fan. Responsive 4-barrel carburetion, special high-speed, dual breaker ignition, solid valve lifters and special valve springs . . . a few of many features for high output capability.

6. Thunderbird 6-V/406 High-Performance V-8— 405 hp. Spectacular acceleration and top speed with three matched, synchronized 2-barrel carburetors; special manifolding, low-restriction exhaust headers. Extra-high capacity oil and fuel systems. Galaxie's top powerplant and a high-performance prize winner.

Ford's 1963 Galaxie brochure showed high performance, race-tested engines among choices available for daily driving.

The 1963 Chevy Impala SS version had special wheel covers and its engine size was displayed just ahead of the doors.

1964

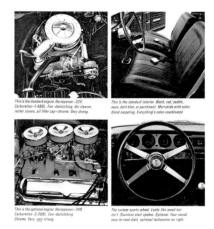

This is the standard engine. Horsepower—325. Carburetion–1 4BBL. Fan–declutching. Air cleaner, rocker covers, oil filler cap–chrome. Very strong.

This is the standard interior. Black, red, saddle, aqua, dark blue, or parchment. Morrokide with nylon blend carpeting. Everything's color-coordinated.

This is the optional engine. Horsepower–348. Carburetion–3 2BBL. Fan–declutching. Chrome. Very, very strong.

The custom sports wheel. Looks like wood but isn't. Stainless steel spokes. Optional. Four round, easy-to-read dials, optional tachometer on right.

Above: *Introduced in mid-year 1964, the Mustang created a stampede to Ford dealers.* David Lyon

Left: *An array of performance features met practicality as buyers discovered the wonders of the Pontiac GTO during the 1964 model year.* Phil Hall Collection

1965

Right: *Chevelle's Z-16 name may have seemed part of the popular secret agent genre but Chevy fans enjoyed it on the street and dragstrips in 1965.* Phil Kunz

Below: *No need to explain what "G-r-r-r" meant to the man or woman on the street in 1965. GTO said it all.* Phil Kunz

1966

Below: *There was another sloped back car from Chrysler Corporation by 1966, the exciting Dodge Charger.* Phil Kunz

Ford's Mustang increased interest with its GT version of the 2 + 2 fastback. Phil Kunz

Left: *Dodge put out a new R/T edition in 1967 as drag racing and street versions got closer than ever.* Phil Kunz

Below: *The Camaro was something new and exciting from Chevrolet in 1967, especially in SS 396 convertible trim.* Phil Kunz

Left: *If you wanted your Camaro on the spicy side, the Yenko version was ready for for street or strip in 1968.* Phil Kunz

Below: *A new face on the scene in 1968 was the unique AMX from American Motors.* Phil Hall Collection

Above: As *if power and sporty trim wasn't enough, Plymouth offered a convertible version of its GTX in 1969.* Phil Kunz

Top right: *Pontiac's Firebird turned heads in 1969, especially the 400 version.* Phil Kunz

Bottom right: *AMX wore the national colors in 1969, complimented by period popular red-striped tires and steel wheels.* David Lyon

Chapter 11

LIGHTWEIGHT
CARS FAMILY TREE

Origins through 1941:

It has always been a part of racing. Losing as much standard car weight as possible to help make the most of the engine's power has always been the practice to increase speed through better aerodynamics and better power to weight ratio.

At the 1904 Automotive Trade Show in New York, people were talking about several lightweight racers. One was Henry Ford's 999 racer.

On Jan. 12, Ford's racer set a new record that was trumpeted around the world, a 39-2/5th-second mile run on frozen Lake St. Clair near New Baltimore, Michigan. "This is 6 and 3-5 seconds faster than the best previous World's Record," touted a Ford ad.

"It was so bitterly cold that Mr. Ford could not keep his foot on the throttle," read a Ford account. "In some cases, the car bounded into the air, jumping a distance of fully 30 feet."

Was it Ford's 999 the first car to do a wheelie or become airborne?

The Ford Motor Company notes also said 1,000 people witnessed the event and that the new record officially surpassed a mark set at Dourdan, France.

The famed Ford 999 racer was an early 20th century record setter.

Not to be outdone, the lowly Alden Sampson Mfg. Co. of Pittsfield, Massachusetts, decided its display ad, across from the Ford in the auto show directory, featured the Sampson 3A four-cylinder car "stripped of fenders, tonneau and hood" and featuring a whopping 16 hp.

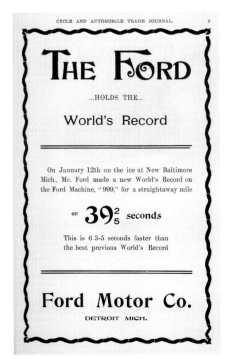

Far Left: *A Ford performance ad, 1904 vintage.*

Top Right: *The 1904 Sampson 3A lightweight stripped of many body parts.*

Bottom Right: *The 1904 Stevens-Duryea racer, a low-slung early lightweight.*

In the same trade journal, the Stevens-Duryea racer, so low the driver sat hunched over a center mounted steering wheel, praised its achievement at a place called Eagle Rock Hill and its ability to win every event it entered.

On Dec. 31, 1903, the Stevens-Duryea racer claimed a 57-and-1-5th-second mile at an Ormond Beach, Florida racecourse.

There was something else in the 1904 show that drag racers would notice.

The 1904 Phelps Touring Car showed how light and easy it was to care for with a picture of its fully opened, hinged body raised 45 degrees, revealing the engine, transmission and frame—some 62 years prior to the famed 1966 Logghe-prepared Mercury Comet dragsters.

Almost as soon as the automobile was offered, some were working on making lighter cars. By 1901,

for example, German blacksmith August Horch had worked on aluminum engine and an aluminum transmission casing. Horch formed his own auto company in 1904.

More than 60 years before the Logghe Comets of 1966, Phelps hinged its touring car body.

Up hill climbs, across frozen ponds, over cross-country treks, in city to city racing, through long endurance contests, around dirt oval tracks and in other early forms of racing, unneeded weight and unnecessary body parts were shed in the pursuit of lightness and speed.

Cross-country endurance tests would proclaim the durability of various cars. The 1907 Thomas Flyer became an early legend in the 1908 New York to Paris competition. Instead of its normal metal fenders, the Thomas used lighter canvas wheel well covers supported by wood.

The 1909 Alco had little above the frame but its covered engine, two bucket seats, a steering wheel, a gas tank behind the driver, twin spare tires and hangers where fenders and running boards had been. The chain-driven Alco looked *de rigeur* for racing of the era.

Dirt track racers were popular as early as the 1910s and it was common to see cars without fenders and running boards, headlights, their large windshields and other features as the cars roared around creating choking dusty clouds. The driver and engineer leaned through curves in these lightweights.

Popular Model T Fords were lightened and modified for racing. One Model T Speedster earned a reputation racing in 1914 as the "Black Widow." In the 1920s, Fords with modified engines also became famous like the Rajo or the Frontenac (or "Fronty") Fords.

Endurance also was a reason to brag about cars. Many manufacturers set out to prove themselves through various endurance tests.

In 1923 an Olds Six traveled "Coast to coast in high gear!" as the ad screamed. The 12.5 day trip from New York to Los Angeles with road racer "Cannonball" Baker at the wheel was intended to show both stamina, "engine flexibility" and economy.

Studebaker often drew attention through its endurance tests. In 1926, a Studebaker was driven

The 1909 Alco was as simple and light as it could be.

from New York to San Francisco in 86 hours, 20 minutes on a 3,471-mile course. The next year, a Studebaker Commander was driven 25,000 in less than 23,000 minutes.

In 1927, Cadillac's elegant sibling, La Salle, tried to quickly prove its mettle by stripping away its Hispano-Suiza inspired fenders, windshield and other accoutrements. "Big Bill" Rader turned heads by driving an average of 95.3 mph in a 950-mile endurance test.

Forward thinkers considered the balance between lightened cars and lighter engines in the 1920s. By1926, *MoToR* magazine quoted the prophetic Fred Duesenberg on the subject.

In early racing competitions, both the driver and mechanic leaned into curves.

"I'll tell you, there are going to be motors traveling at unheard of revolutions per minute before the next 500-mile race, and many of the discoveries that will come out of the engineering laboratory in perfecting these smaller type motors will be in evidence in the passenger cars of the next few years."

In 1927, a Duesenberg Special—imagine a very stripped Duesie fitted for racing and not the country club—was touted by Ross Steering for its victory at the Indianapolis 500. It's narrow body, engine up front and outboard wire wheels were standard fare for the era.

By 1932, practicality added to the mix in a Depression-burdened America. Trying to prove their 2,000 pound Essex Terraplane was durable and practical, an open version was raced up Mt. Washington while a sedan leaned into a dirt track curve.

"What a car!" claimed Hudson after logging more than 660,000 miles of "Terraplaning roadability."

It made sense that early drag racers would follow the trend to reduce weight in order to gain speed, especially since the car owners had tight budgets. The cars they found were used or hand-me-downs.

Early drag racer Tom Spaulding once mentioned he made a profit on a $5 Model A roadster because

In the 1920s, Ford Model Ts were stripped and Frontenac speed components were added creating "Fronty Fords."

he found three cents under a seat cushion while he owned the car!

In California, drag racing grew from Los Angeles area car lovers who competed with their Model Ts, Model As and other makes at dry Lake Muroc and elsewhere, 100 miles or more away.

Their Rajo, Frontenac, Riley, Crager, Miller-Schofield and Dryer enhanced engines made the competitions fun. Later, Ford Model Bs and V-8s competed. Winfield cams and Muncie transmissions were added. The early lightweights were roadsters and touring cars stripped of fenders, grilles, headlights, back seats and bumpers.

Personalities soon evolved from those with the best abilities to experiment and create.

Mechanic Ed Winfield was well known in California racing circles for his Model T special racer. Under the raked engine covering of Winfield's Ford were special ingredients that propelled the car to speeds of 132 mph on a board track and also gave it endurance in 100-mile dirt track races.

As early as 1921, Winfield was working on updraft racing carbs, special fuel injection systems and improved racing heads. His expertise went into the Gilmore Lion Special racer and in the 1930s, and designed a cylinder head that beat larger cars. The Winfield cam became a legend.

While Winfield contributed to drag racing's speed capabilities, men like Tony "Kong" Jackson headed to the Southern California dry lakes for racing, a

practice that had gone on since the 1920s. Four clubs, the Road Runners, Ninety Mile an Hour, the Glendale Sidewinders and the Throttlers formed the Southern California Timing Association (SCTA) in 1938.

"Before that," recalled Jackson, "guys were getting killed at the lakes and were running into each other."

Lightweight racing meant stripping the hot rods, roadsters and touring cars as much as possible.

"We took the windshield and headlights and put 'em in a pile. In those days people didn't steal 'em. We put a tarp on and got in line. I think we ran about 109 mph..."

In addition to removing body parts, Jackson says the early lightweights experimented with fuels and offered an example of a friend who drove to the site.

"...he'd run alcohol at the lakes. When he got ready to go home, he'd drive it 'til it ran out of alcohol and screw the needles in and put gas in it."

"Kong" Jackson was known later for his competition heads, ignitions and manifolds for flathead V-8s.

Other early drag racers included the innovative Spaulding Brothers, Tom and Bill. They began racing at the dry lakes in 1934. Their first Ford V-8 engine was recovered from a wrecking yard in 1936. They designed a pre-war dragster that combined lighter weight and aerodynamics. Riding on a 91-inch wheelbase, the "Carpet Sweeper" used an Essex frame and a sheet metal body. It resembled later Chaparrals.

"…the streamliner was a great drag car," said Tom Spaulding. "We challenged all comers at our Orange Grove dragstrip near our home in Glendora, California."

After World War II, the Spauldings ran a 1,375 lb. car with a 300-hp engine at 140 mph on the Bonneville track in Utah.

The Spauldings became famous for their ignition systems that were "Guaranteed Not to Cut Out," a problem with early dragster engines at high rpms.

In 1940, driver Bob Rufi showed the potential of lighter weight and sleekness with his streamliner

Studebaker used light roadsters for an endurance run from the 1920s.

Above: *A streamlined late 50s dragster.*

Left: Economy and *lightweight design were highlighted in this 1932 Essex Terraplane ad targeted to car dealers.*

Essex Terraplane, with wide open throttle, rounding Dead Man's Curve on one of the fastest dirt tracks of the country—a striking exhibition of stability and roadability

662,766 Miles of TERRAPLANING
Foreshadow Profits for You

Recently thousands of Terraplanes left a single city for cross-country flight. Some destinations were as far as fifteen hundred miles away. The combined total mileage of this severest road test ever to introduce a new car is given in the headline.

Paved roads — gravel roads — dirt roads — winding roads — hilly roads — no-roads-at-all — were covered by these Terraplanes at record-breaking speeds.

In every single instance these cars established a new-day roadability — a distinctly ESSEX

TERRAPLANE roadability — that you can appreciate only when you, yourself, have Terraplaned on the toughest piece of going you can pick.

But don't be content with this, or any other written information about Terraplaning. Get behind the wheel of a Terraplane and convince yourself. Then write or wire for particulars about the Terraplane franchise. There hasn't been an opportunity like this in the last ten years. Hudson Motor Car Company, Detroit, Michigan.

ESSEX TERRAPLANE

What a Car! —and the lowest- $425 and up,
priced Six in America! f.o.b. Detroit

© 1932, Hudson Motor Car Company

that included an enclosed cockpit bubble, a rear-mounted 1925 Chevy four-cylinder engine, an Oldsmobile head and Model T pistons. It ran at speeds of 143 mph.

Said pioneer drag racer Bob Stelling, who raced from 1935 through 1939 on the dry lakes:

"We'd go out on Sunday morning and take the race cars. We used to race on Lincoln Boulevard, too. That was pretty wild!"

NHRA founder Wally Parks began going to the dry lake tracks in 1928.

"…it was run what ya brung," he recalled. "Everybody was out there runnin'"

One problem faced by the drag racing crowd was getting to the dry lakes—often made

dangerous on the back roads at great speeds. At the lakes, the early drag races were akin to a stampede with multiple cars racing, not at all like the parallel competitions of today.

"It was fine for the leaders but dangerous with all the dust for those who followed," recalled Parks.

Ingenuity and creativity produced innovators like Winfield, "Kong" Jackson and Stuart Hilborn, who developed racing fuel injection systems. Vic Edelbrock Sr. built experimented with manifolds and later developed his own business. Tom Spaulding became an ignition specialist. Brother Bill went to work for the Ford Motor Company. Ed Iskenderian became a well-known engine specialist.

These pioneers of speed used ingenuity with whatever they found, were able to buy cheaply or fabricate. Their thinking and experiments would be a great influence in years to come. Prior to World War II, drag racing was well on its way to popularity.

Post World War II:

As the world focused on the tumult of war, drag racing was set aside for several years. Those who would return to the sport would be living in a changed country and world.

In the post World War II era, technology (often including war-time inventions) was beginning to quickly influence everything automotive. Americans

Above: *By 1957, manufacturers were finding ways to produce lightweight racing cars like thie two-door Chevrolet nicknamed "Black Widow."* Mike Mueller

Right: *A powerful Corvette 283-cid V-8 in this 3,100-lb. car predicted great things on the horizon for both drag and stock car racing.* Mike Mueller

had a great deal of can-do confidence and a desire for personal freedom. And the increasingly good economy offered both decent jobs with fair wages and planned time off.

It all fed the growth of a new and dynamic American culture where past limitations were being obliterated. And a big part of the new culture was the automobile.

The car culture was changing as the cars became more plentiful, especially as young drivers and young families took to the roads. And throughout the 1950s, the car became tied to personal and family expressions of achievement and identity.

While their parents and grandparents were constrained with one practical sedans or touring car, driven only around town or to church on Sunday, a new generation wanted all possibilities—speed, power, color, styling, accessories and variety. Two or more cars per family became common.

Americans could choose from an increasing kaleidoscope of models, foreign and domestic. They were pushing for economy and safety at the same time they wanted cars with more style, speed and power.

Returning veterans from World War II brought sports cars with them and these small, lightweight cars influenced many American stylists as well as the racing community.

Jaguar brought its aluminum-bodied XK-120 to race in Florida and was a sensation. European carmakers Maserati, Ferrari and Mercedes-Benz and others would introduce aluminum bodies, tubular frames and powerful engines in numerous production models.

After World War II, technology and drag racing enthusiasm merged in a 1948 twin streamliner dragster. The body was two elongated tear-drop

Ford also experimented with a lightened race car. This is the rare 1957 Battebird, a modified Thunderbird.
Mike Mueller

Ford's V-8 was a potent choice to put under the hood of the race-prepared "Battlebird."
Mike Mueller

shaped 150-gallon aircraft fuel tanks. The left tank house a Mercury flathead V-8 while the right tank served as the driver's cockpit.

The car recorded a 167.91 mph quarter mile in 1949.

That was just one of many examples of how aerodynamics was influencing drag racing cars and salt flat speed racers.

Returning and novice dry lakes racers also sought better places to compete. "Acceleration races" were held in California at places like the old naval landing strip near Santa Ana, the Goleta dragstrip at Santa Barbara, and the Orange County Airport.

In the postwar period, some who were interested in drag racing or who drove custom cars earned a negative stereotype as wild and untamed drivers who raced in the streets and caused accidents. The nickname "hot rodder" often was a negative image for average citizens.

Street racing would become a major hurdle for the drag racing clubs. The illegal racing offered challenges and opportunities. Groups that had been formed before the war, like the Southern California Timing Association, tried to reel in street racers.

Drag racers realized their fun needed more rules if they wanted to be seen as a growing, fun sport, not something scorned by police and the public. A new publication called *Hot Rod* promoted standardized drag racing rules and a governing body.

They also realized some image "sweetening" was needed and sports clubs often volunteered to help motorists in need to soften their outlaw image.

The efforts helped form the National Hot Rod Association, also known as the NHRA and the American Hot Rod Association (AHRA). With the progressive steps taken by these groups, drag strips were standardized, local officials and police were brought in, safety was emphasized and a traveling public relations caravan spread the good news about drag racing across the country.

In Pomona, California, an 8/10ths mile paved drag strip, part of the Los Angeles County Fairgrounds, was set up by police and other Pomona authorities to bring the dragsters off the street and onto the strip. A police officer joined the Pomona Choppers group as technical advisor.

Soon a portion of an old airport runway in Fontana, California, was set up in similar fashion.

Said *Hot Rod* magazine writer W. G. Brown-Medley in a 1952 story: "The opening of this strip was positively sensational, and the promptness and dispatch with which the events were run off resulted in one of the most efficient drag strip operations in existence."

Racers no longer would be chased away from the dry lakes by military personnel on patrol. Fewer hot rodders would be arrested for drag racing in the streets. As more strips were set up across the country, drivers and others could concentrate on the basics of getting the most out of their cars in an era still using old rules but evolving all the time.

"A slow, rolling start was used," wrote Brown-Medley, "to lessen the strain on clutches, transmissions and rear ends. From the starting line to the first timing light is a full quarter mile. The second timing light is 132 feet beyond the first, and he who gets to the last light first is first."

Weight also became more of an issue. At the dry lakes, weight wasn't as critical since the vehicles could use a long distance to get up to quarter mile speeds. But drag racing evolved into best times combined with acceleration during the 1950s on the shorter tracks. That made it entirely different. Soon

Old coupe bodies were used in drag racing like the '33 Willys in "Ohio George" Montgomery's Malco Gas dragster.
Phil Hall Collection

better components meant standing starts would become the norm.

In the 1950s, light roadster bodies were made of aluminum and fiberglass. Aluminum always was considered in the pre-war era but often was expensive to obtain. Heavier and more plentiful sheet metal was used. Fiberglass production technology offered new sources of lightweight materials.

American designers and engineers watched and learned about advances made that would stretch the possibility of what could be done to reduce weight while still increasing power and speed.

Left: *Drag racing had become a popular sport by the end of the car-mad decade of the 1950s.*

Below: *The Chris Karamesenes "Chizler" dragster demonstrates evolving design in the early 1960s.*
Phil Hall Collection

This 1969 Camaro shows the evolution of the lightened body and drag racing frame in "funny car" style.

Phil Hall Collection

While often trying to seem as if they were looking the other way, manufacturers were involved in competition and experimented in bigger engines and lighter bodies. Plymouth heavily advertised its V-800 with competition ads in 1957. Chevrolet advertised one horsepower per cubic inch the same year. And everyone knew Pontiac was becoming a stout performer.

One example of the interest by carmakers was the '57 Chevrolet Black Widow. The two-post sedan had a severely stripped and lightened interior and was powered by the hottest Chevy fuel injected V-8.

Not to be outdone, Ford went all out with its Thunderbird turned racer, the famed "Battlebird."

The body was heavily modified and stripped inside. A hefty Ford V-8 was tuned to performance standards. Both cars predicted what was to come shortly for factory produced dragsters and oval track stock cars.

Drag racers in this era shared the "sky is the limit" philosophy. Some had budgets to match while others

were extremely resourceful. They all began pushing the envelope to see what ideas would make their cars faster—on and off the strip.

Ideas were rampant. Some teams experimented with aerodynamics. Others tinkered with wheel types and sizes or even the positioning of the drivers. Various engine setups were used and some cars even hit the tracks with multiple engines.

New types of dragsters were built from frames and tubing—with names like "rails" and "slingshots."

As production cars became more powerful, they were raced in nearly stock condition at local drag strips.

By 1959, the factories, that had previously put so much attention into stock car racing, began to see the benefits of drag strip racing. First with easily accessible factory parts, then with special order add-ons and finally, full production car packages, the decision was made to jump in and test the waters.

What the manufacturers may or may not have known was their decision would be part of an explosion of interest in cars that has never really stopped.

The car culture would thoroughly influence the Baby Boom generation in music, clothes and outlook. And the overall youth cultural explosion of the 1960s would reflect on all cars but especially on those who desired cars with individuality and sportiness.

The muscle and pony cars would become the street versions of the lightweight dragsters, often just a few horsepower and speeding tickets behind their drag racing counterparts.

Those who experienced the freedom and pure driving pleasure of those cars or who remembered

Drag racers used modified versions of stock bodies in the A/FX class, like this Mustang.
Mike Mueller

the cars of their youth would come back again and again to them and their offerings of speed, power, individual attention and fun.

A lot of work was done on weight reduction and getting the most power to the wheels in the 1960s. The equation also took aerodynamics, tire construction and wheelbase configuration into consideration.

Chrysler Corporation employees who formed the Ramchargers team added another element when they raised the center of gravity in their cars to get more weight transferred to the driving wheels.

By the mid 1960s, the "funny cars" became the rage. These wild-looking machines seemed like stock cars from a dream and were symbolic of a wild and wooly era in North American culture.

It's no wonder these all out machines were popular.

Funny cars spurred one more tangent of cars that weren't legally competitors in sanctioned drag racing classes but were cars that were matched against other, similar machines. Soon these match racers had tubular frames, unlimited engines with all sorts of fuel mixes and fiberglass bodies.

By 1970, NHRA rules revised their classifications and in 1974, tube frames were allowed in competition (rather than just match racing) with acid-dipped steel bodies so that cars maintained a specific weight.

Throughout the 1970s, '80s and '90s, the automakers would respond with cars that offered many of these characteristics on production vehicles. By 2006, the most outrageous combination of lightweight plus powerful engines turned into world speed record production cars like the Swedish Koenigsegg and the exotic Bugatti Veyron.

Today, buyers can seek many factory-produced levels of the speed, power and weight balance, in cars available. While we may never see the outrageous

factory-produced muscle of the 1960s again, all cars draw from their rich heritage.

In their wake, the factory lightweights revolutionized drag racing and became the icons of a generation that has never tired of speed, power and fun in the lightest package possible.

The power sources were tamed by pollution controls, insurance costs and the need for greater fuel efficiency, but the memory of a Ford 427 Cammer, a blown Chevy or the outrageous Chrysler Hemi packed into cars remained. Today, a muscle-bound Chevelle, a stylish Impala Super Sport, a sporty Plymouth Satellite, a chiseled Comet or even granny's shiny red Dodge make every Walter or Wanda Mitty think about heading to the line and watching the lights turn green.

A few have no qualms about spending tens of thousands of dollars to try to preserve a few relics of this famous past.

Your trip to the local grocery may not be the finals of the Winternationals, but your drive will be more fun thanks to all the people and all the technology that produced your car. Its heritage is shared with the wild rides and amazing feats of the Factory Lightweight Era.

Chapter 12

LIGHTWEIGHT
THE HERITAGE

You've probably seen one or more from the series of commercials. A pair of younger drivers in awe of the performance of a Hemi-powered vehicle, like a new Dodge truck, plus the hint of a classic Mopar product in sight. Something always happens to make the jaws of the Hemi worshippers drop in reverence.

This planned homage to the lightweight era is an attempt to recapture past greatness and pass the identity on to the new models. Often, these are cars that might get lost in the automotive marketplace. The identification, such as the Hemi connection, links the product today with high standards set in the lightweight era.

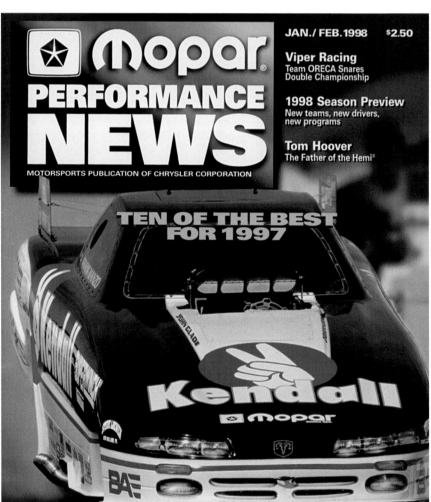

Mopar Performance News featured John Glade's Dodge in 1998 drag racing action.

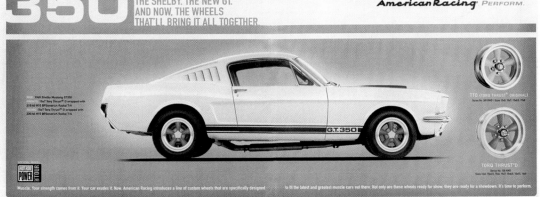

American Racing Wheels used both 1960s and modern Shelby-Mustang GTs.

Below: *Chrysler Corporation highlighted the evolution of racing performance in this Mopar parts ad.*

In a period of efficient, front-wheel-drive, four cylinder sedans, a retro look or even a retro feel can make a lot of difference for both veteran and first-time buyers. One of the mightiest retro directions is to bring back the aura of performance and fun that marked the lightweights in the 1960s. Several manufacturers have already gone in that direction, bringing back names, designs and directions that hearken back to the period of lightweights and production muscle cars.

Of course, much has happened in the 40 to 45 years since those wooly beasts first rumbled to life.

Today's cars have advanced technology and better engineering. The first computer pixel that helped form them on a design computer was linked with world-class platform technology. Engines now are lighter but also

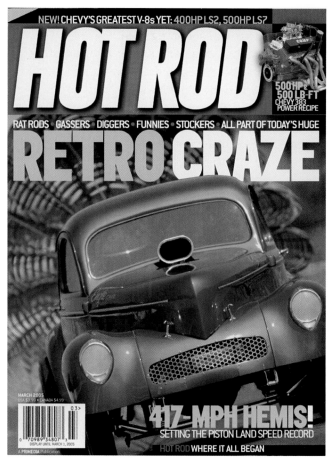
Top Left: *Here's a lightweight Ford Mustang drag racer in a 2005 ad.*
Top Right: *The Hot Rod March cover showed a drag racing revival in 2005.*
Bottom Left: *The exotic Dodge Viper engine was advertised in a 2000 Chrysler ad.*

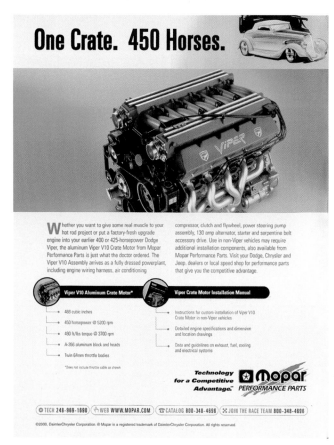
more efficient and even more powerful.

Production methods have changed a great deal from the pre-robotic assemblies of the 1960s with factory lightweights seeming almost ancient to the more quality-conscious standards of the day. Much has been learned about safety and components as well as fuel injection, supercharging and performance.

Modern muscle still offers a high degree of fuel economy never seriously considered with the original screamers of the lightweight days. Also, the ugly duckling pickup truck has grown into a popular, handsome addition in many driveways and is seen more often in fancy dress trim than utilitarian starkness.

Today's consumer may not head to the drag strip with their Dodge Charger or Impala SS but they take to the streets and roads of North America just as their lightweight racing wannabe ancestors did in street performance form in the 1960s. Today's drivers can enjoy sensations of performance motoring while strapping in the family and heading out on the open road or going to the shopping mall.

Step into a new Mustang and enjoy the feeling of the original. All things old are new again. And more may be coming if you've seen the Chrysler Challenger/'Cuda concept or the 2009 Chevy Camaro concept cars.

Lightweights taught everyone valuable lessons about speed, performance, aerodynamics and even gravity. Today's stylists and engineers grew up with those cars in mind and today many have been remembered in either retrospective form or through use of names and characteristics that link the 2000s with the 1960s.

While some would say these great cars have never left us, certainly evident in the examples that come up for auction, others find the contemporary versions pleasing and fun.

Here are profiles of some of these cars:

2006 Chevrolet Impala SS

Today's Chevy SS is remarkably similar in some ways to its 1960s SS predecessors. In fact, *Motor Trend* had some comparison charts on the 1964 SS and the latest edition on their Web site.

While today's sedan is 10 inches shorter than its progenitor, both share similar engine sizes. The 327 of 1964 translates into a 5.3 liter in metric land and compares with today's 303 hp, 5.3 liter (325 cid) engine.

The 1964 mill put out 360 lbs.-ft. of torque available for its rear-wheel drive while the current engine can produce 323 lbs.-ft. of torque and is a front-wheel drive design.

Both cars weighed in at 3,600 pounds with the 1964 SS carrying 60 extra pounds. While Chevy buyers were used to getting either a two-speed Powerglide automatic or a four-speed manual transmission in the 1960s, today's version comes with a tough four-speed automatic.

The 2006 version is 3 seconds faster in the 0 to 60 range at 6.0 seconds versus 9.0 seconds for the 1964 SS. Today's Impala SS has done a quarter mile in 14.3 seconds at 98.1 mph.

In 1964, buyers wanted the open feel of a two-door hardtop and enjoyed Chevy's faux convertible roof and swept styling. One glance at any angle told the average person it was a Chevy.

Today's Impala SS mirrors the age of the Euro-sedan. Practical and aerodynamic, yet fast and sporty, it fits almost any need and every situation. It's too bad the price of the 1964 Impala SS isn't available to consumers today. At least one inflation calculator puts its $2,947 cost at about $18,000 today—good value then as now. Today's Impala SS is in the $28,000 range.

In 2006, the Chevrolet Impala highlighted its versatile sedan format.

The Camaro Concept borrows from the look of the original late 1960s Camaro.

It comes with such goodies as a supercharged V-8, upgraded audio, aluminum wheels, leather seats, and a performance equipment package.

Other Chevrolet SS models include the Monte Carlo SS, with a large V-8 also available, and the much smaller Malibu Maxx SS with a 3.9 liter V-6 that produces 240 hp.

In 1964, Chevrolet attached an Impala convertible's shell to a helicopter and placed it on Promontory Point in Utah for a famous TV commercial. Wonder if the current SS will repeat the feat? Then as now, the SS name means something special when its attached to a Chevrolet.

In 2006, Chevrolet released the Camaro concept car. It may mean more of a good thing prepared in a style reminiscent of the first generation Camaro.

Chrysler 300C SRT-8

At first glance, the Chrysler 300C SRT-8 seems like a custom ride with its tricked front end and large aluminum wheels. The realization dawns that it's a factory version.

Like cars of the lightweight era from Chrysler, this car is the product of some talented car people who have some racing genes in their blood. In this case, their work center is called Street and Racing Technology (SRT).

To quote *Car and Driver,* "Except for AMG in Germany [the performance arm of Mercedes-Benz] no other factory high-performance group is serving up more muscle or as broad a lineup of vehicles..."

The special ingredient of the SRT Chrysler 300C is under the hood. The new version of the Hemi V-8 recalls the terrors of the drag strip in its beastly 425-hp form. It's even painted in Hemi orange.

They just don't talk about cast iron, forge cranks, reinforced rods and such in this day and age. But Chrysler has done it well and even added some new technologies. For example, this Hemi runs on synthetic oil and sodium is used in the exhaust valves to dispel heat.

Chrysler estimates the 300C can go from 0 to 60 in the five-second range coupled to a five speed automatic transmission.

Some things are a big improvement on the past like 14.2-inch disc brakes up front and 13.8-inch discs at the back. Great springs, shocks, anti-roll bars and Goodyear Eagles all mean a ride and handling that won't bring back memories the slalom run-style dips when cornering like some cars from the 1960s.

LET ENGINE COOL BEFORE KISSING.

CHRYSLER

INSPIRATION COMES STANDARD

CHRYSLER 300C. The inspiration: Zero compromises. The result: A powerful presence that makes no apologies ▸ 5.7L HEMI® V8 with 340 hp ▸ Multi-Displacement System provides up to 20% improvement in fuel efficiency* ▸ Electronic Stability Program ▸ CHRYSLER.COM, 1.800.CHRYSLER ▸ 300 starting at $24,200!

'300C as shown, $34,200. MSRPs exclude tax. *17 city/25 hwy EPA est. mpg. From 5% to 20% improvement, depending on driving habits. Chrysler and HEMI are registered trademarks of DaimlerChrysler Corporation. For more information about Chrysler Financial, ask your local dealer.

★★★★★ FIVE-STAR | HIGHEST GOVERNMENT FRONT-IMPACT CRASH RATING

Inset: Chrysler promoted its 300SC SRT-8 in 2006—a powerful engine in a modest sedan.

Left: The 300C version was less sporty but still carried innovative styling.

Like the great 300s of the past, less is more in terms of glitz and glitter with this Chrysler as with its forebearers. There was something about the site of minimal chrome and glitz that always has meant calling attention to its performance on the road. The modern 300C SRT-8 is no different.

The price for a modern 300C is approximately $39,000.

Dodge Magnum and Charger

The original 1966 Dodge Charger was a fastback that looked like a stylist's dream car. Both the 2006 Charger and Magnum have that look as well with their sloping roof lines, especially in the Magnum, a car that would have been placed in the station wagon category in the lightweight era.

Today's Magnum and Charger are creating as much excitement as their namesakes did two generations ago.

There's one big advantage to the "Is that thing a Hemi?" loyalists versus those in the lightweight era. One source says just 468 Chargers ever really were powered by one. The vast majority used the 318-cid or 361-cid V-8s.

Today, that thing under the hood really is a Hemi, at least it's a much more available option.

The 2006 Hemi is a 5.7 liter V-8 that produces 340 hp and 390 lbs.-ft. of torque.

The Magnum offers an SRT edition that comes with the 6.1 liter Hemi and produces 425 hp and 420 lbs.-ft. of torque. Worthy of its name, the Magnum has hit 104 in 13.4 seconds in testing and has gone from 0 to 60 mph in 5.0 seconds.

Like the Chrysler version of the SRT-8, the Magnum carries stiff springs and shocks and large brakes. Inside, the Magnum eschews the Spartan look of 1960s Hemi cars. It has leather and suede furnishings, a 180 mph speedometer, a multi disc CD

In 2006, the Charger emerged once again but in dramatic sedan styling, not a sloped fastback.

changer, Sirius satellite radio and more.

Talk about the lightweight era influence. It's come almost full circle in this power-packed Dodge. It offers the convenience and cargo amenities of the older style station wagons but style and swoop plus power to please most performance addicts.

Once upon a time, the Hemi-Charger wasn't a car at all but a race prep package that made 1964 and '65 Dodges and Plymouths into drag racing champions. Later, it became a classic of the era, a car with trendy style and power aplenty.

That heritage has been reborn in the latest Chargers and Magnums—powered by Hemi engines crafted from modern design and engineering. Then as now, having a Hemi around has always meant something for drivers and admirers.

The Hemi Magnum stretches into the upper ends of $30,000. The Charger sedan is priced slightly lower. A Rip Van Winkle from the '60s would feel comfortable today waking up and getting behind the wheel of either car.

Above: *Dodge hearkened back to its lightweight era performance past with this smokin' 2006 Charger.*

roadandtrack.com

BMW M5 & M6: V-10 POWER PLAYERS

Volvo C70 Convertible: FLIP-TOP FUN FOR FOUR

ROAD & TRACK

Dodge Challenger Returns

Fast Company for the Mustang!

Special Section:

You may think it's the lightweight era all over with this 2006 Dodge Challenger concept.

Ford

Maybe it's lineage of Henry Ford and Barney Oldfield. Performance always has been a part of the Ford mystique.

In the lightweight era, Ford products were memorable from the Lightweight Galaxies at the beginning of the decade to the ground-pounding Torinos toward the end of the era. In between, Ford cars like the Thunderbolt and the drag-prepped Mustangs were performance kings of the strip and Ford translated their prowess to even more memorable street editions.

Today, that heritage is ongoing, even in this era when Ford trucks dominate a truck-hungry era.

Ford products continue to be exciting and innovative. And some link the past and present well.

One is the Five Hundred sedan. While it doesn't have a huge V-8, it does have a large interior and trunk and the name brings back memories of pre-lightweight Ford cars that were NASCAR racing legends.

Another is the GT, a throwback to the mid-1960s GT-40 cars in some ways, with all the improvements and advancements of modern technology. The new GT from Ford is designed as a lightweight and was intended to weigh just 2,300 lbs.

The Ford that really connects with the lightweight era is the Mustang GT, a car that more than any other vehicle in this era of retro vehicles, would have been comfortable and acceptable two generations ago. It has an incredible resemblance to Mustangs of the 1960s and comes with a 300-hp V-8.

In addition to looking right and its allegiance to power, the Mustang's spoiler, canted rear window

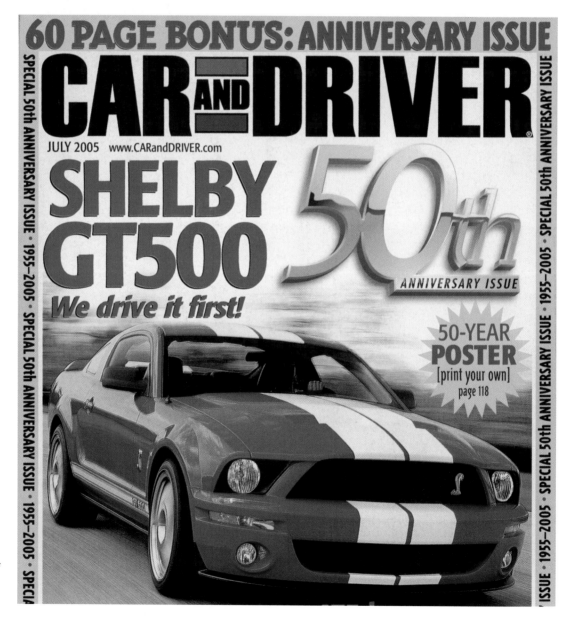

The July 2005 Car and Driver showed the modern version of the Shelby GT-500.

LIFE

LIFE IN [D]

221-hp V6* • Up to 32 hwy mpg** • Class-exclusive 6-speed automatic transmission† • More innovation from Ford
*Optional on SE and SEL. **EPA estimated 24 city/32 hwy mpg (14/automatic transmission). †Class is midsize sedan.

Ford

THE ALL-NEW
FUSION
fordvehicles.com

Ford's "world car," the 2006 Fusion shows how far design and engineering have come.

and healthy rumble make it seem like the great days of the '60s are back again.

The current edition of the 4.6 liter (281-cid) V-8 used in the Mustang produces 300 hp at 5,750 rpm and uses a 3.55 by 3.54 bore and stroke to produce 320 lbs.-ft. of torque at 4,500 rpm.

Like Mustangs of the classic lightweight era, this one has rear-wheel drive.

While the originals used three- and four-speeds as well as Ford-O-Matic, the current V-8 Mustang comes with a Tremec 3650 5-speed transmission. The current edition of Mustang comes with rack and pinion power steering, four-wheel power disc brakes and has a 107.1 inch wheelbase.

In 1966, a Mustang two-door hardtop weighed in at 2,488 lbs. and was priced at approximately $2,400. The fastback edition weighed 2,519 lbs. Today's Mustang weighs in the 3,500 lb. range depending on options. You can get a new Mustang GT V-8 for approximately $27,000.

Pontiac

In the 1960s, Pontiac turned drag racing on its head—initially with the factory made lightweights with huge 421-cid V-8s. If that wasn't enough, they went on to produce the revolutionary GTO, less size, more power and with a popularity quotient that went off the charts.

Pontiac has continued to be a performance oriented automaker, even as others have lost their nerve or wilted from the pressure. Cars like the Judge, the various Firebirds of the '70s through the '90s and more have kept Pontiacs on the minds of those who like performance but still mind their budgets.

In recent years, Pontiac has continued to strive to lead the performance pack in one way or another.

One car that brings everyone back to the 1960s is the GTO. It's the same idea in a modern package— performance plus power at a price that still is affordable at approximately $32,000.

Today's GTOs ride with either a 350-hp or a 400-hp V-8. That's the kind of boost drivers have almost forgotten in a production car.

A new reason for BMW and Porsche to worry.

Pontiac dominated the Daytona Prototypes in the first two Grand American Rolex Sports Car Series races, and is looking to do more of the same in the GT Class with the GTO.R. Like its prototype and 400-hp production GTO brethren, this Pontiac is designed to do one thing: Win. The first-ever GTO.R. **Designed for action.**

©2005 GM Corp. All rights reserved. Pontiac® Pontiac emblem® GTO® GTO.R™

PONTIAC GTO.R

Top Right:
Pontiac tapped into its rich lightweight racing heritage to position the 2005 GTO-R.

400-HP GTO

©2004 GM Corp. All rights reserved. Pontiac® Pontiac logo® GTO®

Right: *The name was revived but the 2005 GTO failed to revive the lightweight era magic.*

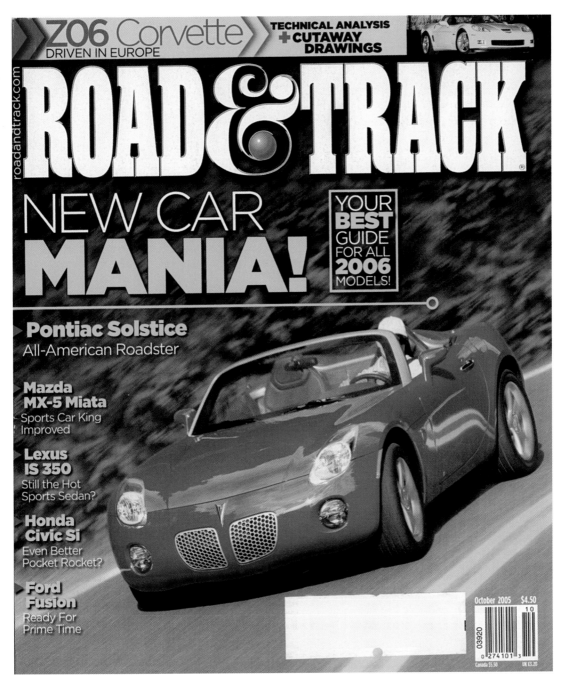

ZO6 Corvette
DRIVEN IN EUROPE

TECHNICAL ANALYSIS
+ CUTAWAY DRAWINGS

roadandtrack.com

ROAD&TRACK

NEW CAR MANIA!

YOUR BEST GUIDE FOR ALL 2006 MODELS!

▶ **Pontiac Solstice**
All-American Roadster

Mazda MX-5 Miata
Sports Car King Improved

Lexus IS 350
Still the Hot Sports Sedan?

Honda Civic Si
Even Better Pocket Rocket?

▶ **Ford Fusion**
Ready For Prime Time

October 2005 $4.50

Canada $5.50   UK £3.20

Contemporary engineering and lessons from the lightweight era influenced the 2006 Pontiac Solstice.

Pontiac always was good at pushing the envelope as well. If it wasn't their use of the Tri Power V-8 in the late 1950s and early 1960s, it was the wider track or the factory-built Super Duty series of cars. And if that wasn't enough, they hit the mark, not only with the GTO, but with the Grand Prix, Firebird and 2 + 2 in those days gone by.

Now Pontiac has prepared a two-door roadster called the Solstice, reaching back to the Tempest roots with a four cylinder engine and a head-turning package.

In this case, the roadster is priced at about $20,000, has a 95.1-inch wheelbase and comes with a 5 speed either manual or automatic depending on one's knack for shifting.

Like so many of the great Pontiacs of the past, this one carries on something directly from the lightweight heritage—a three-letter word called fun.

It is something the performance people never forgot on the way to speed and success.

Even modern drag racers share in the advances made in 1966 by the Logghe-designed flip top dragsters.

Today's cars all have something developed or perfected in the era of the factory lightweights including bodies, transmissions, chassis structures, suspension systems, fuel delivery methods, and reliability.

While they seem very different, modern cars have much in common and much to be thankful for from the cars produced in the lightweight era.

LIGHTWEIGHT
DRIVERS OF FAME

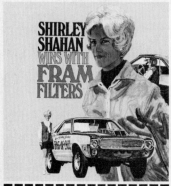

Above: *Shirley Shahan in a Fram Filters ad*

Above Right: *Shirley Shahan and her husband, H. L. Shahan*

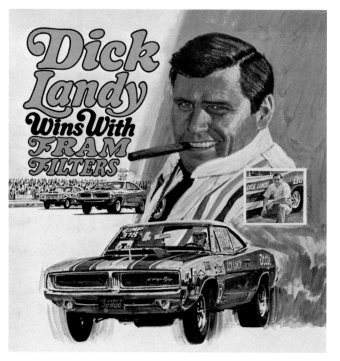

Malcolm Durham

Dick Landy in a Fram Filters ad

Above: *Dick Brannan*

Above Left: *Gas Ronda*

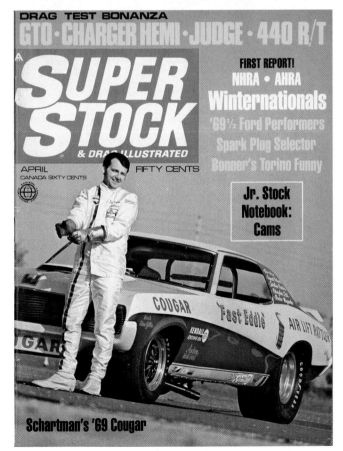

Above: *Ronnie Sox and Buddy Martin*

Right: *"Fast Eddie" Schartman*

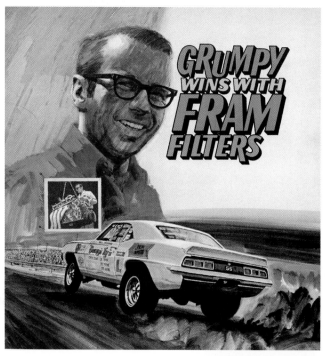

Above: *Bill "Grumpy" Jenkins*

Above right: *Roland Leong*

Above: *Racemaster Tires, circa 1962*

Richard Petty was a drag racer. too.